MODERN
DISPLAY
TECHNIQUES

MODERN DISPLAY TECHNIQUES

by

Emily M. Mauger

FAIRCHILD PUBLICATIONS

New York

Copyright © 1964 Fairchild Publications
Division of Capital Cities Media, Inc.

Ninth Printing 1980

Standard Book Number: 87005-045-1
Library of Congress Catalog Card Number 64-18578

Printed in the United States of America

To
MOSSER
Mine, and her mother's
favorite

Contents

8

CONTENTS

A Forethought

The word "display" may be an addition to the reader's daily vocabulary, but in reality its only newness is the manner in which it is used in the retailing field today. Display techniques have been a part of civilization in one form or another through the ages. Each past civilization, each race, has displayed or shown itself for history to record the good, the evil and the beautiful.

To consider but one civilization in this regard, the Romans displayed their best qualities in their deep philosophy of the theory of why things were as they were. They displayed the evil of their natures magnificently in the amphitheater arenas, in their persecution of Christians, in their chariot races. They displayed their appreciation of the beautiful in their architecture and sculpturing which has lasted through the ages to intrigue engineers and artists. On and on the various civilizations have gone showing themselves for all to see—through the Middle Ages, the Elizabethan, Victorian and Napoleonic periods, down to Gandhi and the Modern era.

Each aspect of history takes the old, the past, adds a bit of the new to it, and presents all for posterity to see and record. Each component part of progress—science, art, education, religion, trade—looks to the past for guidance.

The Gothic arch is just as sturdy an architectural design today as it was in Teutonic times. The basic principle of the wheel may be found today in the yo-yo, the automobile or the phonograph player. Textile mills call upon their vat dyeing specialists to produce colors that were used in the Victorian era, or pixied patterns of wallpaper prints copied from the Edwardian period. Milliners study the Egyptian culture in museums for jeweled effects to superimpose on the modern chapeau. Fashion designers look to the Chinese dynasties for the mandarin collar, the cap sleeve, the coolie coat. Furniture experts bring the Colonial period into the American home of today with cobbler-bench coffee tables, lazy-susans or antique mirrors. Each designer is vying with the other for different ideas or new trends to entice the individual—the customer.

Subsequently, each retailer parades or shows these ideas, these products, to the public for scrutiny, for use, for enjoyment and for posterity to evaluate and record. It is not at all strange, therefore, that merchandising men realize the importance of better techniques for the presentation of these designs, ideas or trends for public trade. The end product of all this show of merchandise, buying and selling, is a livelihood for everyone. And the exchange of goods has been, and is today, the basis for a stable business economy.

American business economy has passed through many exciting phases. It has learned by trial and error the importance of competition, assembly-line production, and the rights of the customer. The strides forward in the retailing of merchandise that have already been taken in the twentieth century seem almost incredible. To appreciate the progress in exchange of goods and to understand more clearly the display techniques of today, one should revert backward a decade or two to glimpse the background of this field and trace its place in retailing through the years.

EARLY AMERICAN DISPLAY

Perhaps the earliest merchant in America was the Colonial craftsman who lived and worked very often within the confines of his own shop, displaying his wares on hooks, tables and shelves. He usually retailed his own products, standing them out front or showing the customer samples of his work. He took special orders only. Such craftsmen had no need for display techniques to sell their merchandise. Demand for their products far exceeded the supply.

As backwoods areas became more thickly settled and craftsmen sought to increase their production with apprenticeship help, the general store came into being, with its pot-bellied stove and shuttered windows. The general store merchant gave little thought to display. He combined storage and display, using the packages the goods came in to show the customer what he had to sell. Cracker barrels, milk cans, cannisters and wooden crates were his fixtures. Display was to him a waste of time and space. His main purpose was to show everything he had and sell it by sight, touch or taste.

The general store merchant sometimes found it necessary to set up barriers between his customer and the merchandise; thus counters and cases came into being. These were placed near congested areas. Shelves reached towards the ceiling, and the whole interior of the store had the appearance of a warehouse. The effect was monotonous and forbidding. The demand for goods still exceeded the supply.

With the advent of mass-production machinery, merchandise became more abundant. Women began to do much of the buying, youngsters were given more liberties, and merchandising entered its most daring and most modern phase in America—competition. Each store was competing for the patronage of more and more customers. One store stood next door or across the street from another store. There was a definite need for a more dramatic presentation of merchandise in order to sell it.

THE WINDOW TRIMMER

As a result, around 1900 most stores began to hire what was termed a "window trimmer." He was the beginning of the profession now called Display. He was a man of many jobs, with seldom enough time to concentrate on any one of them. Part of the time he sold merchandise, as did the other clerks in the store. At night, or when there was a lull in sales, he "dressed" or "trimmed" the windows along the store frontage. He had little help, meager equipment and almost no budget. He was often surpressed by the frugal owner regarding any startling or original ideas he might have for showing the merchandise. The window trimmer made a valiant effort to do the best possible job with what he had at hand, and from this small beginning, display fast became an integral part of the American business economy.

Store interiors and their use for display purposes were ignored almost completely. White walls were broken in their monotony only by the black smudges over radiators or the mop splashings above the floor boards. Stairways were creaky and dark, and the store ledges were stacked high with stock boxes.

Jerome Koerber of Strawbridge & Clothier, Philadelphia, might well be called the father of interior display as it is known today. He was one of the first to do elaborate interior settings for promotions such as his "Florida Show" of 1912.

DISPLAY TODAY

Almost every city in America is now blessed with modern retailing establishments, beautifully designed and ready to serve each customer. The term "window trimmer" has yielded to the increasing responsibility and dignity of the display field until, gradually, it has been replaced by "display man," "visual merchandiser," or "display artist."

Today the job of creating a unique personality, or store image, for the retailing establishment is much more complicated than it used to be even a few years ago. Then almost any shop was able to attract customers by the excellence of the individual items it sold and the way they were displayed. Not so today.

First of all came the discount house which firmly disdained most concepts of store image and display. Its magic appeal was price. Now the discount house is showing that it too can play the game of display, and that the effort is well worth the results. It is beginning to look and act just like a department store while maintaining the low-price image as its main feature.

Secondly, the whole new concept of suburban retailing through the growth of branch stores in shopping centers is a definite challenge to the older downtown stores. The parent store's display director may find himself with a downtown operation and as many as four or five branch stores to supervise and plan and buy for during a promotion.

Display has indeed become big business. But no matter how big it may become, the object of every person in this field is to show merchandise and enhance its selling qualities through methods of grouping and lighting, and with the aid of color and attention-catching devices. Trimming a window or an area sounds like a purely decorative aid to making a store look enchanting, but it incor-porates much more than beauty in its scope. It fosters suggestive or creative selling of merchandise in all types of retailing establishments.

Displays become indispensable to competitive merchandising only when they attract attention, interest the observer and prompt him to action—to buy. Display attempts to show merchandise so dramatically that it becomes a part of the prospective customer's life even before he has purchased it. Successful display is no longer a matter of how *much* merchandise is shown but *how* it is shown.

Part I

THE *HOW* OF DISPLAY

1 The Physical Plant That Is a Store

Each year more metropolitan areas dot the topography of America. Row-houses and crowded tenements are as much a part of such areas as palatial town houses and supper clubs; as, indeed, are the corner drug store, the large suburban shopping center, or any of the retailing establishments up and down the street. Cities are a maze of sharp turns and traffic signals. Buildings rise abruptly from the sidewalk; parking meters stand as so many regimented soldiers along the way. It is relaxing, therefore, for the individual shopper to find a store structurally different from the surrounding network of steel, brick and glass. The prospective customer wants to feel at home where he shops; he loves a change and enjoys anything which is a challenge to his intelligence or personality.

A store's personality is clearly shown by the way it chooses to display itself—from the bargain basement to the top floor, from the front door to the rear entrance, and all along the way.

THE STORE FRONT

Each type of retailing establishment has its own problems—the suburban store, the self-service market, the bakery, the automobile dealer, the exclusive shop. But whatever the type of store, its sidewalk appearance or front will fall into one of three general classes: *arcade*, *straight* or *angled*.

The straight front: The basic rudiment of store frontage is the straight front. This type of structure parallels the sidewalk, with only entrances to break its monotony. The entrances may be recessed into the main floor area, but all the lines are characteristically identical. (See *Figure 1.*)

The angled front: The second classification of store front types, the angled front, is much like the straight front in that it follows a true line, but the monotony is relieved by angles away from the sidewalk contour. Angled fronts may be symmetric or off-center in design with regard to doors or windows. They tend to lead the passer-by towards the entrance and often have deep lobbies which allow traffic to slow down without being shoved or pushed. (See *Figure 2.*)

The arcade front: Arcade fronts are usually quite spacious. This frontage type allows the window shopper to amble around the outside of the store, off the sidewalk, and scrutinize merchandise more closely. Arcade fronts may be very open in sweep or more complex with island-type windows placed amid their expanse. They seem to be more relaxing to the shopper and often take on highly surrealistic shapes with concave or slanted panes of glass and beautifully decorated windows. (See *Figure 2.*) Windows are the eyes of any store, and they deserve careful consideration.

Many suburban stores with off-the-street parking lots are giving less and less attention to display windows along their frontage. The explanation is that their shoppers park in the first vacant space and seek the nearest entrance. Many such stores overcome this lack of ability to influence the individual with window displays by placing huge display areas directly inside the entrances or

Lord & Taylor, New York

1   STRAIGHT STORE FRONT

where there is heavy traffic, such as near elevators or escalators.

A fascinating innovation fostered by city beautification committees is the mall or promenade core for shopping centers. These core areas, often with partially-covered walkways, have fountains, benches and meandering courts as well as board, terrazzo-edged, landscaped malls. Here the displays and windows are most influential upon the passer-by in his selection of a store to shop and patronize.

DISPLAY WINDOWS

Where there are display areas along the store frontage, they are identified as *elevated, elevator, ramped, lobby, shadow box, corner, island,* or *open-backed* windows.

Elevated windows have a usual floor height of from twelve to fourteen inches above the sidewalk level. This is mostly a safety measure to protect the expensive glass panes from damage by scuffling feet, clean-up crews and vibration caused by passing vehicles. A floor of this height also helps get the displayed merchandise closer to eye-level

where it can be seen more easily. Some stores have elevated windows with floors twenty-four to thirty-six inches above the sidewalk to accommodate the type of merchandise sold. Jewelry stores, book shops, optical stores and bakeries fall into this category. (See *Figure 3*.)

Elevator windows are the display man's dream. They are so desirable because their floor level may be raised or lowered at will. They are also very expensive to install since they involve a complicated hydraulic system. Such stores as Lord & Taylor in New York City and Fashions in Houston, Texas, are shining examples of the dramatic use of elevator windows. Under this type of window set-up, display departments are usually located in the basement; the windows are lowered one floor, trimmed and then raised to the desired elevation. (See *Figure 4*.)

Ramped windows are actually only a variation of a standard window. The main difference is that their floors are slanted or elevated in the back to form a ramp-like display area. Such windows facilitate showing merchandise attached to a panel. Any window may be made a ramp window merely by installing a false floor with its back edge higher than the front. Many bakeries, banks, utility buildings, shoe shops and drug stores employ this type of window for their displays. (See *Figure 5*.)

Lobby windows: Just as its name implies, this kind of display area follows the lines of deeply recessed entrances to buildings. Lobby windows are usually slightly angled to help lead the customer right into the store. They present a display problem since people must be attracted coming and going as well as straight on. (See *Figure 6*.)

Shadow box windows may be small and an entity in themselves or they may be a segment of a larger window which has lost space due to a structural block. Grill work, unsightly pipes, posts and doorways are camouflaged very nicely in frontage layouts by the placement of shadow box windows. Also, they afford a display area for

Lilliputian merchandise such as jewelry, toys, cosmetics, notions, books, handkerchiefs, infant shoes, etc. (See *Figure 7*.)

Corner windows are often considered the most important areas of any store frontage. They are the central viewing point of converging traffic and are consequently the very best of merchandising areas. The average pedestrian will notice a corner window and its contents much more readily than he would a side street window.

Stores value their corner frontage to such an extent that they allocate their finest merchandise and their very best decorative pieces to it. The store front of Herpolsheimer's of Grand Rapids, Michigan, is most unusual. At one end of the building a large section of the structure is almost entirely glass, extending from the sidewalk level to the top of the building. Sears, Roebuck in

Angled

Arcade

2 ANGLED AND ARCADE STORE FRONTS

Stern's, New York

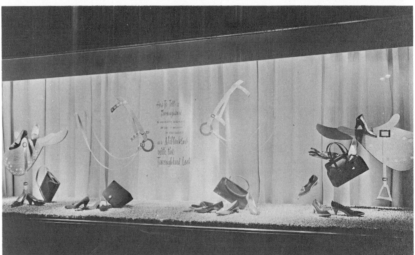

I. Miller & Sons, New York

Whitehouse & Hardy, New York

3   ELEVATED WINDOWS

Lord & Taylor, New York

Lord & Taylor, New York

4   ELEVATOR WINDOWS

B. Gertz, Jamaica

B. Gertz, Jamaica

5 RAMPED WINDOWS

6   LOBBY WINDOWS

Baltimore, Maryland, has a corner window which reaches two stories high for greater attraction.

Island windows are almost self-explanatory. They are usually found in arcade fronts and are isolated from the rest of the building. This type of window offers many display problems because it can be seen from all sides. Merchandise must be placed so as to appear just right from all angles.

Open-backed windows: Most store windows are separated from the rest of the street floor area by complete partitioning—ceilings, floors, side and back walls. However, there has been a trend since the end of World War II, both in remodeling and in new building, toward opening the store to full view of sidewalk traffic. Thus far the trend has been confined more to the smaller stores, but whether there is to be a definite swing toward open-backed windows remains to be seen. Many retailers have found that this type of window stimulates and invites the passer-by to come in and look around. Properly handled, open-backed windows become quite effective. Replacing the lost stock and storage areas and maintaining effective displays without blocking a clear view of the store are but two of the problems which arise here and require added ingenuity on the part of the display man. (See *Figure 8*.)

Windows, whether they be ramped, elevated or open-backed, are the store's invitation to enter. They may have stopped the customer and enticed him to turn in at the front door. Certainly their presentation of merchandise identified the store and indicated its prestige. But good display does not stop at the nearest entrance. The interior of a store must continue the impression that the front windows create. The shopper in the building is the most valuable asset the store has. Every means of making that visit pleasant is an investment in sound business practices. There is no worse disappointment to the esthetic nature of a shopper than to come from strikingly chic street windows into drab, uninspired main floor or departmental interiors.

DISPLAY WITHIN THE STORE

Displays inside and outside a store should be related. It is elementary to speak of good directional signs or related merchandising patterns or functional stairways, yet they are just as important in getting the customer to the product as a full page of newspaper advertising or a fifteen-second TV commercial. They are necessary elements of display. The whimsical mural showing a boat with Wynken, Blynken and Nod aboard on the infant's department wall is as much a part of good merchandising as the well-designed fixture, the adept clerk, or the corner window. And so, departments, shelves, counters, ledges, cases, display areas and the furnishings within the peripheral walls of a store demand analysis when considering proper display techniques.

All furnishings of the store should be placed so as to enhance the visual impression each floor of a store presents to the customer. They should be arranged to sell the most merchandise and at the same time be pleasing to the customer. The attraction-ratio of a store's layout, with regard to its

Lord & Taylor, New York

Bloomingdale's, New York

7   SHADOW BOX WINDOWS

W. & J. Sloane, New York

Rogers Peet, New York

8 OPEN BACK WINDOWS

Stern's, New York

9   CORNER SHOPS

Miller's, Inc., Knoxville

10 COUNTERS AND TABLE DISPLAYS

furnishings, should be improved wherever possible. It should never remain static.

Placement of store furnishings can easily be coordinated with the needs of the customer and those of the store. If it is early spring and time to feature outdoor grills and cookery of that type, counters and tables may be moved to allow an outdoor terrace effect. If the yuletide season is approaching, consideration should be given to moving store furnishings to accommodate Santa and his throne. Teen department furnishings may be arranged to resemble the corner drug store on the first day of school, or campus fashions promoted with a "college board." Any change which will increase sales is an important step to consider, from the merchandising and display viewpoint.

Corner shops and marked-off places with a distinctive decor are sometimes employed by store engineers to relieve the sameness of departmental furnishings. These shops lend color to the appearance of the department, and they often become meeting places for customers. (See *Figure 9.*) In a large store it would be difficult to find one person on the fourth floor; but if that one person said that she would be at the Young Elite Shop for business women, the Jewel Box of Millinery, in a Baby Boutique, or at the Magnolia Room to eat, she could be more easily located. Also, while

she was waiting she would naturally look about the designated area. A clerk, meanwhile, might start a friendly conversation with her. The person waiting might even decide that her wardrobe should include some of the merchandise displayed there. She would thus become a customer—impulse shopping at its best.

Shelves: Anything which adds to the pleasure of buying relieves the monotony of buying and thus increases the volume of sales. In order to increase sales volume, there must be a volume of stock. Shelves are necessary for this purpose and are a definite part of the store furnishings in every department. Shelves are poor display areas. They should be hidden wherever possible by walls, curtains, or masks of interesting design and color. If they are all that is available for showing merchandise, then the display man should be very critical of them. He must keep them spotlessly clean. He must be sure they do not sag in the middle. He must keep them devoid of unsightly nails, thumb tacks, soiled paper, or streaked paint. Removing a shelf at intervals will create a shadow box. Painting shelf areas light pastel colors, making them of various heights, widths and arrangement patterns, slanting some of the shelves, inserting an oval-shaped shelf occasionally amid the row-upon-row of straight lines, and using a quaint

11   INTERIOR LEDGE TREATMENT   *Lord & Taylor, New York*

design across the corners of one section of shelving will tend to relieve the crowded appearance of stock areas.

Counter and table displays sell merchandise more readily than shelf displays because they are located in front of the stock areas and therefore bring the goods nearer to the customer. The customer may feel and touch the merchandise on a table or counter. (See *Figure 10*.) Square and rectangular shapes are the accepted design for counters and cases. However, rounded, oval, and surrealistically-shaped counters ease the flow of traffic through a store. Display areas with rounded corners appear less regimented and do not present sharp edges for the customer to come against unexpectedly. They are a pleasant change from the squareness of design which the shelves present.

One arrangement device which will increase sales, at no added expense to the store owner, is placing store furnishings at an angle to the structural lines of the interior. Even a slight deviation from the usual parallel-to-wall place-

ment will lead the customer around the store more comfortably and more leisurely. If all aisles are straight from front to back, the customer moves too quickly through the store. Any change in the line of the furnishings will slow the customer and invite him to take notice of what he is passing. Likewise, when the customer is leaving, counters carefully arranged at angles to the wall will seem to hold him back, to reduce his speed in going. Each hesitation on the part of the passer-by is an opportunity for interior displays to make a sale.

Shadow boxes are often located behind counter areas. They are easier to work with in setting up displays than counters or shelves because they are generally well beyond the reach of searching fingers or pushing elbows. It is a great deal easier to maintain a preconceived arrangement of merchandise in a shadow box, but here a more dramatic presentation than that used on counters is required to overcome the customer's inability to handle the merchandise. What a customer cannot comprehend by touching the merchandise must now be shown vividly. Shadow boxes are larger than their name would imply, are in many instances enclosed with glass and are often very cleverly designed. Shadow boxes are illuminated with side, ceiling, or indirect lighting of greater intensity than their surrounding areas so that they will attract attention immediately.

Ledges—the tops of shelves—sometimes serve as areas for display. They necessarily follow the set structural lines of a department. Ledge areas may be made very attractive with the addition of decorative pieces for seasonal promotions. (See *Figure 11*.) Ledges, having shelf space under them, are above the comfortable range of vision. Because of this, constant care must be exercised by the display man in the placement of merchandise. Unsightly portions of certain merchandise—chair seats, shoe soles, wrong sides of materials, unfinished backs of stoves, refrigerators—should not be visible to the customer's eye and must be camouflaged with decorative effects.

Island areas, as their name implies, are isolated display places amid the pattern of shelves and counters which constitute the principle selling space of a store. They are forceful merchandising agents when placed strategically at elevators, near entrances to departments and at stairway landings. Island displays catch the customer's fancy and attract the passer-by's eye. They are not stock areas, nor should they be crowded with boxes and signs. They are concerned exclusively with showing merchandise and/or items related to that merchandise. They may be built from five to twenty-eight inches above the floor, may or may not have a background, and are often finished with carpet, grass, linoleum or wood. They are well illuminated and allow space for figures, forms and other fixtures attendant upon the showing of merchandise.

All store furnishings, of whatever description, should complement the impression desired for a certain section of a store. Plush covered pouffs would be out of place in a toy or camp equipment department. Glass shelves are much more practical for jewelry or handbags than they are for heavy cans of paint. Island display areas are desirable for children's apparel departments, but sectional room displays are far more useful in furniture departments. As the needs of a department change, the store furnishings should be converted to meet these needs, whether they be sectional or seasonal.

The importance of store furnishings cannot be over-emphasized when considering the impression a store and its wares make upon the public. Furnishings lead the customer through all departments; they provide the clerk with areas for stocking, showing and selling merchandise; they serve as feature display areas to attract the customer. Furnishings—their type and placement—play a leading role in the dramatic presentation of merchandise.

2 Upright versus Landscape Display

When every effort has been made to have the store and its furnishings—the windows, the cases, the shelves, the shadow boxes, etc.—arranged to best advantage, then consideration should be given to the commodities these furnishings are designed to sell. How is the merchandise to be placed with the highest selling quotient in mind?

MERCHANDISE CONSIDERATIONS

Many otherwise excellent displays are marred by the addition of just a few too many articles. The selling potential of displayed merchandise does not depend upon the amount of goods shown but upon *how* they are shown. Too much merchandise grouped together in an area will tend to repel the customer. Crowded displays seldom stimulate impulse shopping, but properly spaced merchandise with an attractive background becomes alluring and charming for the customer.

Nevertheless, the display man's axiom is always: "What is seen, sells!" Much of the appeal of store display is through the eye. Eye appeal is responsible for 90 percent of impulse sales. Display is largely responsible for eye appeal. A customer's side glance picks up some bright color or novel placement of merchandise in a display, and that momentary pause, for no matter how short a time, causes him to be attracted and to be pleased or displeased. Thus the need for choosing the most appropriate arrangement pattern to fit each display situation is of paramount importance.

The appropriate arrangement pattern for merchandise on display amid the maze of store furnishings is influenced by the customer's point of approach to the display as well as by the merchandise itself. Will the display area be seen first by the customer turning a corner, getting off an elevator or stepping from an escalator? Can the area be seen from all four sides or will there be a structural background? Can the customer's glance be attracted from a distance? Will the merchandise be shown to better advantage in an upright position or should horizontal landscape design be followed? The answers to such questions determine whether merchandise should be placed on a high plane, on a low plane, at sharp right and left angles or parallel to the background, on a ramp, suspended from the ceiling, *ad infinitum*.

The eye level of an arrangement pattern is also the display man's concern. Eye level is that point or height which is even with the eye of a given individual at a given time. (See *Figure 12*.) Some individuals are tall, others short; some customers will be standing when viewing a display, others will be seated. Consequently, a median eye level should be found for each display and all arrangement patterns in that display should be built around that level.

The arrangement of the display is made so that the weight of its component parts will be at or below comfortable eye level. If more traffic will view a display while walking by than while sitting down, the eye level of the arrangement should be adjusted accordingly. In the event that it is necessary to have some parts of a display slightly above or below eye level to carry out an effect, the

12   EYE LEVEL

normal eye path is diverted to the highest or lowest points by the use of a bright color, a draped piece of material, or a concentration of light.

Merchandise shown on the same level or in a straight line is monotonous. Merchandise should never be shown flat when it can be displayed otherwise! Varying planes and angles are used advantageously to relieve monotony within an area. The usual eye movement over a surface, such as a written page or a counter or a shadow box, begins at the left and, traveling in an arc, swings upward and then downward, almost completing a circle. (See *Figure 13*.) If it is allowed to follow

its usual path, photographing the area seen, the eye takes into its visual field every part of an area. This normal movement may be diverted and led in another direction by any abrupt change in line or color.

The merchandise itself is the next essential in considering arrangement patterns. Here the display man must decide how the merchandise to be shown will be worn or used by the customer. If the merchandise has any special features, such characteristics are accentuated in the display. The plaid lining is shown dramatically; it is pointed out that the socks have elastic tops, that the shoes are wedgies, that the blade is stainless

13 USUAL EYE PATH

and for the best possible showing of the merchandise in stock.

Pyramid arrangement is the easiest pattern to use and is particularly helpful in crowded areas. It is geometric in design and often follows the lines of a perfect triangle. The pyramid begins at a large or broad base and progresses up to an apex, or point, at the highest level. (See *Figure 14.*) This type of arrangement is used vertically as well as horizontally. Merchandise spread out in the back of a display becomes smaller in arrangement pattern as it comes to the apex in the front of the display, or it follows the true Egyptian pyramid pattern vertically. Cereal boxes stack easily blockwise in this pattern; paint cans are well-suited to this display construction. A pyramid shelf displayer helps to improve the effect of pots and pans which have been merely stacked in each other before. Stacked display areas quickly lose their monotony if the natural or unexpected is introduced: lift the collar, puff the sleeve, spill out some soap flakes, knock over a bottle or one can of paint.

Zig-zag arrangement is a modified pyramid pattern. The main difference is that, in reaching its apex, no two heights are the same. Zig-zag arrangement begins at a broad base but apparently gets lost on the way and zigs or zags toward the top. (See *Figure 15.*) For example, consider three pairs of shoes. Placing them according to pyramid arrangement, one pair of shoes might be in the center of the display at a height of eighteen inches while the other two would be shown at a height of twelve inches, at identical angles and in identical position on either side of the central pair of shoes. In contrast to this simple pyramid placement, the zig-zag arrangement would show the center pair still eighteen inches high, but if the shoes on the right were twelve inches off the floor, the pair on the left side would be shown at a height of fourteen inches or ten inches or, in fact, any height other than twelve inches and below eighteen inches. Use of zig-zag lines does much to relieve the monotony which sometimes occurs when pyramid arrangements have been used to excess in a department. The zig-zag pattern seems to flow and is more graceful; likewise, it is more feminine.

Step arrangement is much like a child playing scales on a piano. It goes up and then it goes down. Such patterns lend a feeling of motion and harmony to a display. Step arrangements lead the eye in a direct line; they begin at a low point on one side of a display area and progress directly to a higher point on the opposite side of that area. (See *Figure 16.*) They do not zig-zag, nor are they

steel, that the glass bowl may be used in the oven as well as on the table. Anything about the merchandise which might differentiate it from the mass of other merchandise is a good selling point and will indicate, to a marked degree, the arrangement possibilities.

Often certain features of the merchandise itself suggest how it will be shown in a display area. Assuredly an 8′ × 10′ rug could not be displayed to advantage in a small area; but notion items, such as buttons, threads or zippers, could be shown in detailed arrangement patterns.

ARRANGEMENT PATTERNS

The arrangement of items on display usually follows four definite patterns—pyramid, zig-zag, step, and arc or fan. These patterns are used in variation, for a change of pace, for added grace

Kolmer-Marcus, New York

14   PYRAMID ARRANGEMENT

Stern's, New York

15   ZIG-ZAG ARRANGEMENT

16 STEP ARRANGEMENT

Henri Bendel, New York

pyramid in appearance. Because of their linearity, step arrangements are sometimes referred to as diagonal arrangements. The varying heights of crystal glasses available in an open-stock place setting lend themselves especially to this type of pattern; stacks of books on a cluttered sale table, if arranged in a step pattern, will attract more customers into the department. Step arrangements follow the Mother Goose theme of "Papa Bear, Mama Bear, and Baby Bear" with merchandise. They allow room for accessorizing the display in the blank space left at the base of each step, which increases in area with the addition of each rise.

of Valentine note paper might be placed on either side of an upright plastic heart with appliqued Valentine cards.

BALANCE

Formal or true balance is the term used to describe a display in which each half is identical with the other half—everything is balanced on an axis. (See *Figure 18*.) Formal balance lends itself to almost any type of merchandising problem.

Free or informal balance is the opposite of formal balance in display. With informal balance,

Gimbel Brothers, New York

17 FAN ARRANGEMENT

Fan or arc arrangements are shaped like inverted pyramids. They spread out from a small base, much like the tail of a peacock, leading the eye outward and upward. (See *Figure 17*.) Fan or arc patterns are excellent for displaying merchandise such as umbrellas, golf clubs, decks of cards and notion and hardware items. Cosmetics also lend themselves to this arrangement pattern.

Any one of these four arrangement patterns may be used alone or in combination. For example, given a large counter area, a zig-zag grouping

there is no apparent plan of groupings nor is there a central axis of symmetry. (See *Figure 19*.) At first glance, the merchandise appears to have been placed at random in the display area, but this is not the case.

Free balance is more difficult to use than true balance; it requires ingenuity; the merchandise and the setting must be coordinated. Each display should be weighed from the point of view of which balance, free or formal, will best suit the particular setting. Free balance is considered more modern

18   FORMAL BALANCE

than formal balance. Both can be quite effective in displaying merchandise.

DISPLAY CONTENT

Whether using formal or informal balance, the trend in the arrangement of merchandise today is increasingly toward the unit or related display and away from mass displays, which have been and still are utilized in dime stores, drug or hardware stores and discount houses. Unit or related groupings alleviate the monotony of massed merchandise often necessary in such stores.

The unit grouping of merchandise within arrangement patterns employs similar articles or identical items in each display. This likeness may be carried out to the nth degree, or it may become liberal in character. A unit grouping of handbags might consist of all sorts of handbags, all leather handbags, or simply all red leather handbags. Another display might have groupings of three green leather handbags, five black suede bags, and three brown faille bags, but they would still all be handbags.

Related groupings, moreover, inevitably present accessory articles along with the featured items. (See *Figure 20.*) If the display of handbags mentioned above relied on related items for a more varied and dramatic presentation, the display might consist of one green leather handbag with a matching belt and billfold, three black suede bags with several pairs of contrasting gloves, and one brown faille bag with handkerchief and flower. Any one of these three groupings might be used independently. Display in related groupings constantly reminds the buyer of his need for more than the central item. This is called suggestive selling. Today more and more selling is suggestive selling.

In unit or related groupings of merchandise, the use of an odd number of items within the groups is considered intriguing to the customer. Odd numbers attract the passer-by; they tend to be restful and dramatic. The display man need only refer to everyday life to see the reason for this: a four leaf clover is an oddity; the human hand has five digits; one week has seven days. Five handkerchiefs, seven fountain pens, or three table cloths are more restful to the eye than four, eight, or two; they are easier to show and they seem to look better when on display. In the event that there has to be an even number of items within the groups, the display man chooses an odd number of groupings for his arrangement pattern. Water glasses usually are sold in sets of six or eight; shoes are sold in pairs. The display man might place five glasses to one side like soldiers, and add to the sixth such accessories as a colored straw, a linen napkin under the glass or a piece of mint hanging over its edge. To the pair of shoes, a display man would add a matching umbrella, or a contrasting handbag.

Blank space or white space, as it is often termed in display, between related and unit groupings of

Bloomingdale's, New York

19 INFORMAL BALANCE

Abraham & Straus, Brooklyn

20 RELATED GROUPINGS

Stern's, New York

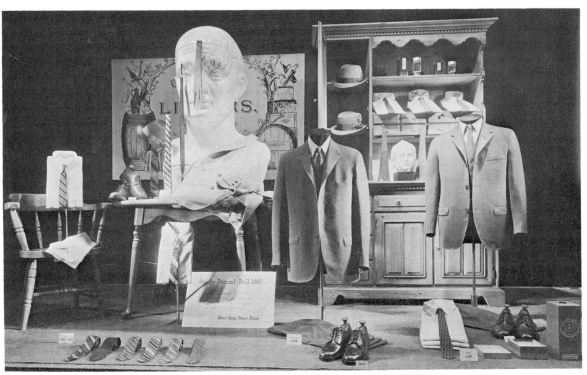

merchandise is very important for quicker perception of the merchandise by the customer. These white spaces tend to accentuate the item on display. An example of how white space adds to perception is this very page of reading matter. Blank space defines the margins, the paragraphs, the sentences, the very words. If the page were covered haphazardly with letters and there were no space between words or lines, the ideas it presents could not be grasped as quickly and in as orderly a manner. So it is with merchandise on display. If used thoughtfully, white space relieves the cluttered appearance of even such mass display items as can openers or extension cords. White space accentuates the merchandise, permits all parts of the display to be seen clearly and in order, and presents a coordinated picture which is an added force on the buying habits of the customer. White space helps to create order out of chaos.

In summary, the display man pursues a course approximating the following when displaying merchandise: (1) he chooses a rectangular, oval or surrealistically-shaped area whenever possible for displaying the various items; (2) he places some of the items in the upper half of the display area but most of them in the lower half, for weight; (3) he arranges some of the items at an angle to the sides of the display area, and others parallel to the sides of the display area, following the usual eye movement over a given surface; (4) he leaves blank space between the groupings of merchandise so that all of the display may be seen clearly; and finally, (5) he considers the balance, the unit groupings, and the arrangement patterns within the area best calculated to relieve monotony. Putting all these things together, the display man will have produced a satisfactory and well integrated arrangement.

3 Fixtures and Their Uses

Since the primary purpose of display is to show merchandise attractively to customers, the question of what to hang the merchandise from, to stand the merchandise on, or to separate the merchandise from other displays of merchandise presents a constant problem to the display worker. Fixtures are the answer to this problem. With them the display man can attain height and perspective. Fixtures are used to present shirts removed from the box, gloves off the counter and piece goods away from the walls.

Fixtures include the many metal, wooden, plastic, rubber, glass, plaster, wire, papier-mâché and upson board items constructed to support and display merchandise. They should not be confused with store furnishings. Furnishings are the more permanent pieces of equipment in a department, such as the counters, the shelves, and the shadow boxes. Fixtures are added to the store furnishings and are generally designed for certain definite types of merchandise. Fixtures give life and contour to the many products placed on them for display. They allow merchandise to be shown at many levels and from all angles; they add dramatic effect to a display. They are of inestimable assistance to the display man in assembling and installing a display quickly. Certain basic types of fixtures are essential if a modern store is to show its merchandise to the best possible advantage.

Variety in fixtures will assist the display man in his flair for theatrical presentations. Fixtures are an absolute necessity for good display. In serving their purpose, however, fixtures should remain inconspicuous. After all, the fixture is not for sale; it is the merchandise on the stand or the form which is being marketed. Therefore, great care must be exercised to choose the most appropriate fixture for displaying a given item. Here again, as in all phases of display, the unexpected is pleasing to the customer's eye. A bird cage far too enormous for the wee canary but filled with lilacs for m'lady's lapel, or the neck of a blouse form painted with pink roses will cause the passer-by to relax and smile. The wire suspending the bird cage will be inconspicuous and the stand holding the blouse form will not be noticed in a proper display picture. The effect of a display must be conspicuous, but the mechanics of it should be indiscernible.

FIXTURE TYPES

Fixtures fall into several general classifications: stands, with an assortment of tops, easels, millinery heads, forms, plateaux, displayers and set pieces. Unless the display man has a working knowledge of these various fixtures, any reference to them, other than a list to show what a well-equipped fixture room should contain, would be lost in technicality. So fixtures are listed here and described briefly.

Stands serve as a basis from which to work in gaining height in display. Because they have adjustable extensions, stands adapt themselves to a variety of fixture needs. Stands are made in several sizes measuring from eight inches to beyond thirty-six inches in height, and many of these

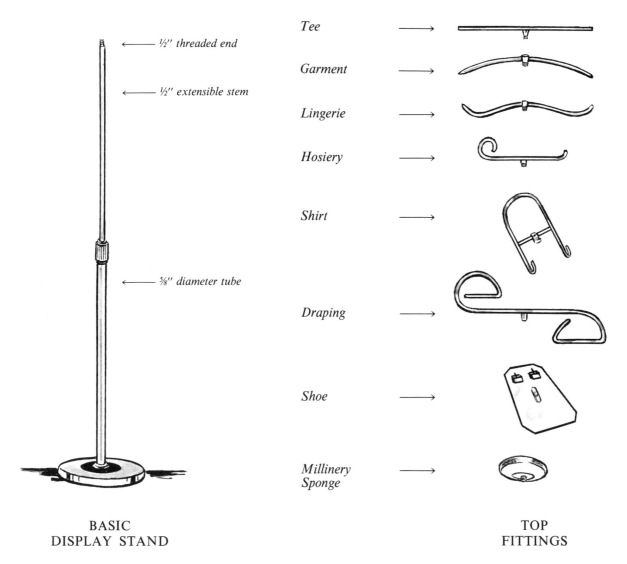

½″ threaded end

½″ extensible stem

⅝″ diameter tube

BASIC
DISPLAY STAND

Tee ⟶

Garment ⟶

Lingerie ⟶

Hosiery ⟶

Shirt ⟶

Draping ⟶

Shoe ⟶

Millinery
Sponge ⟶

TOP
FITTINGS

21 DISPLAY STAND AND TOP FITTINGS

stands have an extension rod which permits doubling that height. Display stands are made of metal, wood, or plastic and may be used to support merchandise, boxes, or background foliage. They have different and sundry screw-on tops to accommodate all types of products and are the most valuable all-purpose fixture a display man may have in any department or store.

The many different attachments and tops which screw on metal stands include the T-top, garment top, lingerie top, balsa wood top and shoe top: these make the stand versatile and a valuable fixture. (See *Figure 21*.) The T-top is a straight utility bar from which scarfs, fabrics, or towels

drape easily; in the larger variety, blankets, rugs and tablecloth patterns are also hung tastefully from the T-top.

Garment and lingerie tops curve as human shoulders do and lend a semblance of human character to the merchandise. Garment tops are used for displaying sweaters, blouses, dresses and jackets. When adjusted to the proper height on the stand they cause the merchandise to assume body form—sleeves hang casually and the shoulders are rounded. Lingerie tops, as their name implies, are used almost exclusively for showing sleeveless lingerie. The only difference between lingerie tops and garment tops is that the ends of the lingerie top turn upward to keep the narrow straps of slips and gowns from sliding off the bar. Shoulder-strap handbags or ironing cords, incidentally, might be shown on this top along with such accessory items as a scarf with handbags and a pretty doily with the ironing cord.

Two other types of fittings for the metal stand are the balsa wood top and the shoe top. Balsa wood tops serve as a base for showing pajamas, shirts, and men's underwear, which are usually displayed folded as they come packed from the factory. The monotony of stack upon stack of sweaters is relieved when one is pinned to a balsa top with a sleeve fluffed up in a characteristically mock-human gesture. Balsa tops are made in rectangular shapes of a soft wood which takes pins easily, and they have an angular adjustment underneath for versatility. Shoe tops are similar to the balsa tops in that they have an angular adjustment which allows the display man to tilt them up or down, thus affording the best possible view of the merchandise. This top makes shoes seem orderly and neat when used in a display and is equipped with steel pins so that the pump or wedge heel will not slide off the tilted top.

Easels are small in relation to other fixtures, even in proportion to most stands, but they are very useful in showing books, boxed stationery, china and glass, cosmetics, handbags, homewares and other small items. They support the merchandise and stand it perpendicular to the display area. Easels are made of metal, plastic, wood, rubber or wire; they are inexpensive and may be used even as a card holder or small shelf support.

Millinery heads are fixtures designed to be used mainly for displaying hats, but they may also be employed to show fur scarfs or jeweled necklaces. Some millinery heads are designed to resemble the human head, with every facial feature apparent; some millinery heads are merely a blurb or oval with no features at all; some are made of chicken wire or covered with newsprint; others are cast in beautiful black or blue glazed china. They are usually self-standing—they support themselves—and they may be used at varying heights when placed on an auxiliary stand. Millinery heads enliven a display, not only because they suggest the human head, but because they add height and depth to the line and arrangement pattern of a display.

Forms constitute the broadest classification of display fixtures. The form category includes full body forms or parts of the body both for the male and female figures. They are made of plaster,

rubber, papier-mâché, lucite, or a non-breakable plastic substance which resembles the human skin in texture and finish. Forms are life-sized and require special attention on the part of the display man when dressing them or moving them about from place to place. Full figure forms are quite fragile and must be handled carefully. They are one of the most expensive of display fixtures. (See *Figure 22.*)

Full figure forms include those resembling men, women and children. All full figure forms have detachable parts to ease the problem of dressing them—their arms and hands are removable and, in the case of children's and especially infants' figures, even the legs are detachable. By moving a hand or an arm, the dressed figures can be made to take a stance suggesting a very real-life situation. The face of today's modern manikin is no longer abstract, immobile, blank. It has character. The hair is plastic, horsehair, cord, or even real and looks very much alive.

Appendage forms, so called because they are a reproduction of the hand, arm or leg in varying degrees of wholeness, are self-standing and, while primarily designed to show gloves and hose, may lend lifelike characteristics to other merchandise. Glove forms would permit the draping of a pearl necklace, or they might show the sheerness of hosiery pulled over a hand. Leg forms may be used for shoes, garters and hose, and are a suitable means for showing the relation of a new fashion hem length to the calf of the leg.

Women's blouse forms and men's coat forms include the torso only; they seek to give an effect of garments shown on full figures, at less expense per fixture, and they are devoid of head or appendages. Coat or suit forms are used extensively for men's wear and are full round. Blouse forms are usually half or three-quarter round and are meant to suggest the front half of the female figure, from chin to just below the hip-line. They are used exclusively for women's apparel and may be attached to a stand, if desired, for variety in height.

Platforms, displayers and set-pieces are other fixtures found in a well-equipped display fixture room. They set the stage for a pleasing presentation of merchandise. Each presentation seeks to be different from the former one. These three fixture types add endless variety to a display man's handiwork. A platform is the riser in a display; it is the floor for other fixtures and, in store interiors, keeps the customer traffic from treading all over the merchandise. A platform is never very high but may cover a large area. It forms the boundary lines for a display or it separates the several types of merchandise used within a single display area.

Displayers, unlike platforms, are sometimes hung as panels from the ceiling, may be used as ramps to segregate merchandise, serve as the background for a display, or simply show merchandise while remaining completely inconspicuous themselves. Displayers are well constructed and their usefulness depends largely upon their being artistically different. They are self-standing, as a shelved Christmas tree displayer, may be hung, as a baroque frame and are often finished on all sides for use on ledges or in other open display areas where they will be seen from several angles.

Set-pieces, as distinguished from platforms and displayers, include such things as small statuettes, foliage, and even telephones; statuettes of ballerinas used as a suggestion that the apparel might be worn to a ballet; foliage used to transplant the outdoors indoors; or a huge antique French telephone used to herald a new Paris fashion. They are the atmosphere pieces of a display. Set-pieces, or props as they are called in the theater, are powerful selling helps, for they dramatize any merchandise setting and add verve to the merchandise picture. They, along with all the other fixtures mentioned, help the display man to present merchandise in an attractive manner for the customer to see. (See *Figure 23*.)

What the customer does not see in a merchandise picture is all the work and preparation required to place merchandise on the various display fixtures mentioned above. Each time a display man shows a piece of merchandise, he follows a definite technique so that he may be assured of the best possible presentation. The display man adheres to a pattern of work and preparation unconsciously and automatically; he knows it must be done the same way each time for perfection in display technique. This backstage work requires a thorough knowledge of the placing of a blouse on a garment stand, of the proper way to dress a mannequin, of the adeptness at hiding price tags, etc.

FIXTURE CARE AND PURCHASE

Before any fixture is used, it is thoroughly inspected and put into proper working condition. Finger smudges must be washed off; lucite fixtures require a periodic polishing with abrasive cleaners to remove collected dirt due to static electricity; metal stands always require a dusting to protect the merchandise used on them from soilage; and many displayers need a fresh coat of paint seasonally. There is nothing which will make a fixture more conspicuous than to use it when it is dirty or broken; and, as has been noted before, fixtures should remain inconspicuous.

Fixtures may be used for several years if carefully handled and neatly stored when not actually in use. To avoid breakage, loss of vital parts or an excessive collection of dirt, they are stored in specially built shelves and cabinets: shelves for plaster pieces, stands and displayers; cabinets for millinery heads and fragile set pieces. Forms and mannequins should be stored in a room by themselves to protect their finish and keep the various parts intact. If they are stored in regimented order and always kept in perfect condition, the display man can see at a glance which fixtures are at his disposal for the display problem at hand.

Most fixtures are expensive. Nevertheless, the initial cost of fixtures is soon recouped by the store through the increased sales that result when merchandise is shown tastefully, attractively and forcefully.

There are establishments whose prime concern it is to design, manufacture and market the different articles which come under the general term of display fixtures and display effects. Display houses present their products under two general categories: finished products—displayers, bird cages, mannequins, commercial murals, etc.—and raw materials—flowers, foliage, papers, rope, rattan, pebbles, etc.

Some firms specialize in mannequins, some in metal fixtures, and others feature displayers or promotional pieces; all gladly give advice and guidance when it is requested and make an earnest effort to help with any special fixture problem which the display man might meet. Often manufacturers offer their line of fixtures in catalogues which they send out seasonally, or they have traveling salesmen who call on display men periodically to show the line. Some of the many sources for fixtures are listed in *Appendix iii* of this book.

DO-IT-YOURSELF FIXTURES

Since budgets are often limited and fixtures are expensive, the problem of assembling dramatic displays with a limited supply of fixtures presents itself to the small display department. Makeshifts are one solution for this constant demand for new settings. Cast-off materials like shoe boxes and cardboard tubes can sometimes be used by the ingenious as substitutes for an expensive fixture. (See *Figure 24*.)

Shoe boxes covered with attractive paper become buildups for imaginative display men. Silk

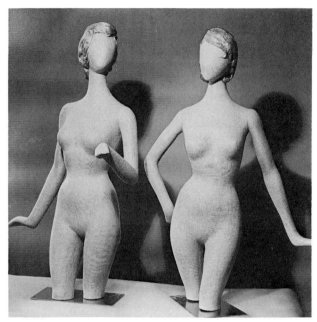

D. G. Williams, New York

Burlap ¾ Figures

Suit Forms

Molded Rubber Figures

Saks Fifth Avenue, New York

D. G. Williams, New York

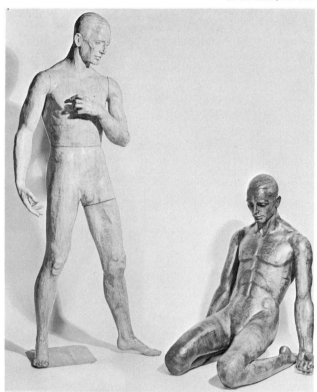

22   DISPLAY FORMS

Art Sculptured Mannequins

Surrealistic Mannequins

Teen Mannequins

22   DISPLAY FORMS

Displayers

23 DISPLAYERS, SET PIECES AND PLATFORMS

Saks Fifth Avenue, New York

Displayer Becomes Set Piece

Set Piece

Stern's, New York

Stern's, New York

Platforms

23 DISPLAYERS, SET PIECES AND PLATFORMS

Tiffany, New York   *Arnold Constable, New York*

Tiffany, New York   *Saks Fifth Avenue, New York*

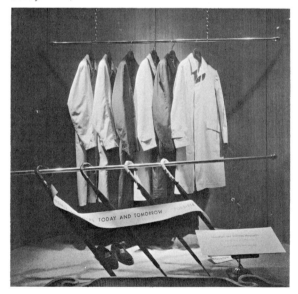

24 DO-IT-YOURSELF FIXTURES

crepe dress goods are wound on tubes, which may be painted pastel colors, and used as stands of varying levels for merchandise (rugs are often shipped wound on unadorned tubes or bamboo poles). These tubes might also be cut in lengths and used as legs to support the shoe boxes. Again, they might be painted white and wrapped candy-stick-style with red ribbon. Finials added to cardboard tubes help them become standard bearers announcing special events. Men's round hat boxes add a curved line to the arrangement of a display. Figures on pattern posters may be mounted and cut out of heavy cardboard to be used in many effective ways with findings and fabrics. Make-shift fixtures are not ideal, to be sure, but they are a help to the display man with a limited budget. They will add variety and spice to an otherwise drab picture.

Often display aids are so close at hand that they are completely overlooked. Consider a furniture outlet: a borrowed piece of furniture is all that is needed in return for a quickie display prop—the hope chest for silver, china, linens, gifts to the bride—the beautiful Boston rocker as a center unit for a toy display, with a bit of metal attached to one rocker blade and a battery magnet motor hidden behind one toy so the rocker will rock slowly back and forth; those bamboo poles shipped with rugs make handsome space killers or even a shop motif if painted Chinese red or bantam gold; the cardboard tubes in which linoleum is transported may be transformed into May poles, flag poles, trapeze bars or fancy barber poles to promote Bon Voyage gifts with only a bit of paint or ribbon.

No city or town is without its hobbyists. Coin collectors love to show the extent of their rareties, petipoint enthusiasts would deem it a lark to show some of their patterns or work. Even the fire department which repairs broken toys for the indigent at Christmas takes pride in presenting the "before and after" aspect of their work. The chain reaction word-of-mouth publicity gleaned from these presentations is well worth the slight bother of invitation and investigation.

Fixtures, make-shift or otherwise, are the very backbone upon which all good display depends. They hold the merchandise up for the customer to see. They are the parts of a display picture which give it height and perspective. They assist the display man in his effort to present merchandise quickly, effectively and dramatically. They provide a setting which causes the customer to associate the items displayed with the very real conditions of everyday life and thus add to their selling-quotient.

4 Color Dynamics Simplified

America is more conscious of color psychology today than ever before in its history. All phases of daily routine are influenced by the use of color, from the comic book's cover to the dentist's office, from the meals Americans eat to the cars they ride in, from the movies they see to the clothes they wear, from the colored cement lanes of the superhighways they drive on to their thought of changing the color of the one, five, and ten dollar bills they use as currency. Being such a dominant factor in the life of the individual, it follows that color holds an important place in the retailing and merchandising field. Color attracts people, stimulates movement of traffic, and sells merchandise wherever it is applied with reason and purpose. Practically everything in a store has burst into color. Even the American male is succumbing to its use in the clothes he wears. The customer is unquestionably becoming more color-conscious.

Clerks with rouged cheeks and platinum blonde hair, wearing bright-rimmed eye glasses, stand near Daliesque glass counters and satin pouffs in departments where walls may be painted light yellow, soft green or any shade of the rainbow. Patterned linoleum floors, carpeted elevators with colorfully-uniformed operators, stairways and escalators lined with fantasy paintings, and bright directional signs lead the customer from one department to another.

THE SCIENCE OF COLOR

Color gives form to every object seen by the human eye—from the giant redwood tree of California to the tiny postage stamp on an envelope. An object is seen when light cast upon it is reflected to the retina of the eye. The color of the object regulates the reflection of light from the object. There is nothing in a yellow second sheet of typing paper, for example, that gives off yellow light. The dye in the paper simply absorbs (nobody knows quite how) the red, orange, green, blue, violet, indigo and some of the yellow light that falls on the sheet from surrounding sources of illumination. The rest of the yellow light is reflected rather than absorbed, so the eye sees the sheet as yellow. In much the same way, the sky appears blue, but not because it is colored that way. A black object absorbs all wave-lengths of light, reflecting virtually none; a white object reflects all colors of light, absorbing virtually none.

Color vision is one of the most marvelous of human gifts. The eyes of an individual are so conditioned by the pleasant blending of colors in nature that he instinctively responds happily to a balanced color scheme and unhappily to color arrangements that clash. Nobody, not even specialists in this area of knowledge, knows too much about what color is, just how it is seen, or precisely what its effects are on human attitudes.

The physical nature of color has been the subject of scientific investigation since Issac Newton passed a beam of white light through a glass prism in 1666 and found that the beam separated into the hues of a rainbow, the visible spectrum. Since then, all sorts of systems and theories of color identity have been set up—the tristimulus system, the subtraction method, the Munsell system of chromas, the Ostwald system, the Young-Hemholtz theory of color vision and many others*—but display need not be too concerned by all this scientific data regarding color. In display, more emphasis is placed upon the simplicity of colors, their influence on the customer, and how merchandise of myriad colors may be shown to better advantage.

COLOR IN DISPLAY

Many books and articles have been written on the theory and use of color and the science of seeing. Not nearly enough, however, has been written on the scientific or psychological use of color in retailing establishments. Few stores utilize the help that correct color schemes can give them. Merchants want their merchandise to be displayed so that the color, texture and other features will be properly enhanced, and sales resistance lowered. Correct color schemes cost no more than incorrect or haphazard color schemes and greatly improve the sales results of any department in any store. Merchants fail to use proper color techniques in displaying merchandise because they think of color as a mystery which they cannot fathom; they are reticent about anything which is new; or they entrust the task to someone without a working knowledge of color who selects colors according to his own taste without considering the store's need or a specific problem.

Examples of color use which follow stress the importance of color psychology for improved sales and customer stimulation.

First example: There might be the store whose third floor—the fashion floor—has been remodeled. This floor had an unusually high ceiling with exposed sprinkler pipes and air conditioning ducts. The new fluorescent lighting system required that the fixtures hang just slightly above a good clearance height of eight feet from the floor, necessitating long suspension rods from the high ceiling

to the lighting fixtures. The ceiling and all pipes and ducts were painted ivory, and the new lighting system accentuated the defects of the exposed pipes. Installing a plaster or metal suspended ceiling proved to be impractical: the costs were great and the fashion floor would be out of business during the remodeling period. The new lighting system had established a plane of light at a fixed level, and it was suggested that all the surfaces above this level be painted a flat charcoal black or midnight blue. An unsightly area was thus eliminated, with the customer feeling at home in more modern surroundings, and the store saved thousands of dollars in construction costs while continuing business without interruption. Color made the difference!

Second example: The proper use of color in merchandising establishments might involve problems concerning the customer's complexion. Fitting rooms are among the chief offenders here. More sales are lost by poor color and lighting in fitting rooms than by poor salesmanship. Too often fitting room areas are painted ivory. Nothing could be worse. After all, most flesh is a muddy color and ivory tones do absolutely nothing for such complexions. They are cruel to the customer and the merchandise. To overcome this fitting room color problem, the wall opposite the mirror should be painted in soft tones of blue-green or turquoise which are the opposite, or complement, of flesh-tones. The side walls could have a pinkish cast to reflect some of this tone in the customer's complexion and figure. In this setting, almost all shades of merchandise will look well on her. For an added dramatic effect, fitting room entrances could be made into colorful beach cabanas to offer a refreshing change from the drab line of "cells" which almost inevitably greet the customer. Color makes the difference!

Third example: Merchandise itself may influence the feelings and responses of an individual in a store. Levi's or blue jeans will do very nicely as the merchandise. This merchandise is blue-black in color and not too dramatic, to say the least. Placed on a pale blue background, the jeans take on a soft quality which relieves the harshness of texture and cut; placed on a soft lime background, the jeans become electric, dramatic, objective; placed on a background of terra-cotta tones, the jeans are in their element of ruggedness and take on added depth. Floral or striped backgrounds would do very little for the tomboy characteristics of this merchandise. Rather, they would detract from the merchandise on which the emphasis should center.

---

*. . . *tristimulus system* identifies a color by combining lights to give the three primaries needed to produce the match.

. . . in the *subtraction method*, light is passed through a combination of transparent standards which subtract portions of the spectrum until a match is produced.

. . . *Munsell system* classifies color according to hundreds of variations in hue, value and chroma.

. . . *Ostwald system* designates color according to its white, black and full color content.

. . . *Young-Hemholtz theory of color vision* states that color arises from combinations of the three responses that the eye can make to color—sensations of red, green and violet.

Some tests conducted by a color research institute showed that:

1. Of those asked to choose a favorite coffee offered them because of taste, over two-thirds made their differentiation on the basis of color of container. The contents of all three cups were the same, yet the green cup won most acclaim.

2. Well over 90 percent of women tasters in a margarine-butter consideration chose the yellow pat to be butter by taste when actually the white pat was butter.

3. Bob, bob white soap suds are now blue because of public demand. Red granules were acclaimed too harsh on the hands; yellow granules did not clean the wash; blue granules proved just right and very soothing besides.

Call it a point of mind over matter. Call it individual taste. In either case, color made the difference!

Color is a differentiating force in human relationships, too. Color of skin often sets up prejudices; the varied colors nature offers in the yearly cycle cause individuals to react gayly in the spring and soberly in the winter. When thinking of white in relation to medicine, there is the picture of a doctor and his kindliness; when relating white to the bride, her sweet fluffiness or the purity of her vows comes to mind. Red has always been associated with firemen and their engines, but it also reminds the individual of lips that are so inviting, the perfection of a rose, the innocence of a newborn babe, or the stop signal on the corner. Children react happily to bright colors. Children always choose stark contrast over pastel tones, while adults prefer soft tones and combinations of color. Men, it has been found, are far less conscious of the colors around them than are women.

The display man cannot possibly hope to please the color tastes of everyone all the time, but he can cultivate the taste of his customers gradually and purposefully. He realizes that the colors people say they prefer and the ones they actually buy will often be entirely different, that during depression periods black and subdued tones predominate, and that as economic conditions improve, color tastes turn toward the soft, the brilliant, the striking and the dramatic.

SIX BASIC COLORS

The first important principle in any study of color is the fixed interrelationship of the six basic chromas. These include yellow, red, blue, green, orange and violet. Every display workshop should have a chart posted somewhere with these six colors arranged for easy reference in planning color schemes, in considering merchandise or backgrounds for a display, and for matching colors already at hand. In the six-color-system there are three primary and three secondary colors. The three primary colors are so called because they are independent in themselves; they cannot be produced by combining other colors to make them. Conversely, the three secondary colors may be obtained only by combining one color with another. Red, blue and yellow are the primary colors; orange, green and violet are the secondary colors.

Red is the most powerful of all colors. It is stimulating and symbolizes cheerfulness and enthusiasm. It is used to greatest advantage in displays for Christmas, Valentine's Day or carnival promotions. However, red is more generally used for accent in display and in small quantities—as a belt on an ensemble, as a check-mark on a white copy card, or as a ribbon leading from a wall-map down to a pair of shoes so that the ribbon's brightness associates the merchandise with the interesting background.

Blue is often thought of as the masculine color. It is associated with the deep blue of the ocean and the light blue of the sky. Its whole being suggests calmness and assurance. Ice blues are excellent for background areas in electrical appliance departments: they contrast the whiteness of the appliances with icy softness, tending to take the warm drudgery out of kitchen tasks. The blue of the sky with a cloud drifting by, the blue of a ripple at the water's edge, the blue of night and all its mystery—each sets up a pleasant association for the customer.

Yellow is the lightest color in the spectrum and is quite naturally considered the sunny color. It is highly stimulating, but if used to excess it becomes fatiguing. Because yellow is more visible at long distances than other colors, it is especially suited to display areas with poor lighting facilities. Yellow is popularly used in displays at Easter and in the spring. It is also a child's color and may be utilized effectively in toy and infant departments. Yellow often adds a precious touch to a display when used in golden tones.

Orange is obtained by combining red and yellow in equal amounts. Pure orange, like pure red, must be handled sparingly in display; it is more pleasing used in shades or tints. Orange is dramatic for harvest scenes and popular in Halloween promotions. Because of its intensity, orange may clash in color combinations. With fashions, orange is suggestive of Mexican Fiestas or Florida sunshine. A carnival sales promotion of summer dresses might be done very effectively with pale orange posters and green tent tops scattered about the department.

Green is the color of nature. It is made by mixing yellow and blue and is probably the most universally popular color. Green is relaxing and suggests softness; it helps to make a small area seem spacious. It soothes the nerves and is a reminder of ordinary, everyday things. Its symbolism carries through well in display—the green of American currency, the go-signal at a traffic intersection, or the newness of life which buds forth each spring.

Purple is a dignified color. It was once worn only by royalty because purple dyes were so difficult to find and purple cloth, therefore, was expensive to produce. Resulting from the equal mixing of red and blue, purple has a dull quality which limits its usage. It reminds one of church windows and the need to step forward quietly. Purple is predominant in displays for the Easter season and lends itself well to animations and fantasies. It is excellent in displays where theatrical effects are desired. Black opera pumps, for example, may be shown to beautiful advantage against a background of crushed purple satin, relieved and enhanced by a cream-colored, fringed shawl.

These six basic colors are usually arranged in what is called a color wheel, starting at the top with yellow and continuing clockwise with green, blue, purple, red and orange. Colors directly across from each other on the color wheel are known as complementary colors. A combination of any two complementary colors will produce a dull, muddy brown. A rich brown results from a combination of red, orange and black. White, black and brown are known as the neutral colors. They are used as moderators when bright-hued colors threaten to clash in a display.

White is the combination of all colors; pure sunlight is utterly white. Black is the absence of all color—the opposite of white. Adding white to a color produces a lightened color or tint; when black is added, the result is a darkened color or shade; adding brown dulls the color. When using colors of various tonal qualities, from the lightest to the darkest, rather than pure values, the picture presented becomes more pleasing to the eye.

COLOR RELATIONSHIPS

The second important principle of color is that colors are constantly in one of three relations to each other: they *harmonize;* they *contrast;* or they *clash.*

Harmony in color is achieved when two or more colors are combined so that they make a pleasing picture. And this is true whether the combination is dramatic: a yellow and a red tulip; elegant: a brown and russet autumn leaf; or subtle: yellow and chartreuse stalks of wheat. Each combination is equally harmonious. Taking merchandise for examples, these color harmonies would manifest themselves in a display of brown leather belts on a bright russet maple leaf plateau with several smaller yellow and brown leaves scattered in the area; in a display of red toy sleighs dashing over snowy white hillsides—each sled laden with men's ties in tones of yellow, brown and garnet as gift suggestions for dad; and in a display of chartreuse ribbons, intertwined about a yellow Maypole, caught by handkerchief dancers in deeper shades of yellow.

At times, the simplest way to attain color harmony is to develop a one-color theme. A scheme based on a single color depends for variety on the use of different intensities of the color and on contrasting light and shade. Given three beige jersey blouses to arrange in a shadow box, the display man might use a one-color theme as follows: beige is a tint of brown (white is added to brown to produce the color beige) and brown had its beginning in red and oranges. He might choose tanbark or terra-cotta papers for a background color in this instance, because these papers both have brown as their base color. A rusty pink or dark brown item, such as a pair of gloves, a belt, a scarf or a rosebud, might be used as an accessory color with the blouses. The result would be a pleasing one-color picture for the customer to see.

Contrast in texture of both merchandise and background also engenders interesting displays; for example, the smoothness of men's silk shirts shown on a dull finish, such as flat painted surfaces or woolen fabric. Soft napped crepe materials drape easily and contrast beautifully against a glossy background, especially mirrors or patent leather merchandise. Jewelry, which in most cases is all glitter and sparkle, shows best when contrasted with short napped materials, as velvets, felts, dark failles, or even burlap.

Clash: The use of colors which clash defeats the whole purpose of display.

The display man will usually avoid discorded colors by careful selection of merchandise. There are times, however, when merchandise items of clashing colors must be placed next to one another. This will occur more often in a small, crowded department where a certain amount of

every item has to be shown. Cosmetic containers often prove to be of clashing colors. Each cosmetic firm is identified by the characteristic color combinations of its boxes, bottles and tubes. To relieve the harsh vibrations and reflections which sharp color contrasts present to the customer, neutral colors and abrupt changes of line are utilized in display. Placed amid the haphazard stacks of suntan lotion bottles, a white baroque frame, featuring a book and perhaps a pair of sun glasses, will relieve the myriad colors in a cosmetic department. Gray material, draped gracefully between a group of red cosmetic boxes and another group of blue cosmetic boxes, will separate the harshness of red and blue used side by side. There are few clashing color situations in a display man's world which cannot be handled properly by forethought and adequate color planning.

Color is a highly dynamic force in life. It affects the mind and the emotions of the customer. It is a vital element in merchandising, and its functions need not be a mystery to the display man. To appeal to the general public, an unsophisticated use of color in display is often quite as dramatic as a complicated series of merchandise paintings. Color is an integral part of each day and every situation, so its use in a store presents a natural panorama of eye-pleasing beauty.

5 *Lighting Techniques*

To be sold, merchandise must first be seen. Seeing is, indeed, the biggest thing in selling. The more a customer sees, the more he buys. True, store furnishings help the prospective customer see what the establishment has to show; true, merchandise can be more easily seen if placed on fixtures and not left lying flat on a table; true, color is dynamic in any picture presentation of merchandise—but what would these elements of display be worth without illumination? Proper lighting can make merchandise more attractive and easier to find; adequate lighting creates a more pleasant atmosphere for the customer to enjoy while shopping; and good lighting invites him to make that store his preferred place to buy.

Light and seeing are inseparable. Light changes the whole aspect of a scene. The type of lighting used in a store may convey warmth, gaiety, or stately serenity. Conditions that make seeing easy and accurate for the customer help to increase the sales volume of a store. A poorly illuminated store becomes just one more in a row, with no individual attention obtained, no character. The shop looks out-of-date. People stroll along past it, and its displays, with little or no concern for what is there. Proper lighting adds charm to a store. Good lighting patterns assure the customer of a detailed and exact picture of the merchandise for sale.

The principles behind the art of lighting in the home, the store, or the theater are highly technical. It is unnecessary to investigate here such technicalities as foot candle level, gimbal placement, or parabolic reflectors.* These problems may be safely left to the engineers and the lighting specialists who plan and install store lighting systems. For display purposes, the analysis of lighting patterns in their simplest form will suffice. The reader should understand that *light* is radiant energy reflecting from an object and acting on the retina of the eye to make that object visible. *Intensity*, in lighting, is the degree or amount of that reflection.

The lighting must be considered in planning a store—beginning with the neon sign out front that identifies the store and going right up the stairways, down the aisles, to the elevators and back to the front door. There are three distinct phases of lighting to consider when discussing store illumination, namely, *primary*, *secondary*, and *atmosphere lighting*. (See *Figure 25*.)

PRIMARY LIGHTING

Primary lighting supplies the bare essential of store illumination. Outside, it includes the 150 watt bulbs used as basic window lighting, the marquee lighting which illuminates the sidewalk for the window shopper and the lobby ceiling

---

* . . . *foot candle* is a unit of measurement used when determining the intensity of illumination at a particular spot.
  . . . *gimbal placement* refers to a type of lighting fixture which allows free movement of the bulb in any direction.
  . . . *parabolic reflectors* are conic receptacles for incandescent light bulbs. They resemble a funnel or sauce pan upside down and are often highly polished for added reflectance.

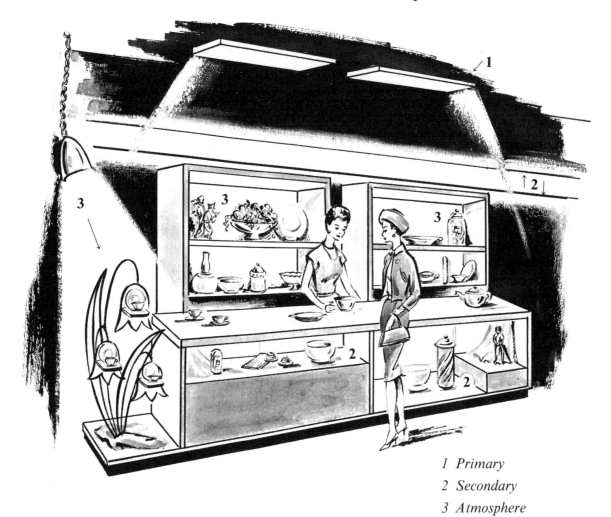

1 *Primary*
2 *Secondary*
3 *Atmosphere*

25   SHOWCASE LIGHTING

lights. Inside, primary lighting provides general illumination for the store, including lights along the aisles, an indicator on an elevator, the light in a stairway, and a directional sign at the fire exit, the office, or the down-going escalator. This general illumination is the minimum adequate store illumination.

Primary lighting may be fluorescent or incandescent, direct or indirect, depending upon the need of each type of store. Automobile showrooms require bright, concentrated light to accentuate the chromium trim of a new car and the beauty of its paint job. Bakeries employ indirect light to emphasize the soft and brown tones of bread and pastries. There is not enough space here to consider each store situation, but almost every city maintains a lighting engineer as a public service; his advice is available for the asking. Also, lighting fixture salesmen will offer many suggestions, and there are reams of ideas and suggestions to be had in pamphlet form from manufacturers— General Electric, Westinghouse, Lustre, Sylvania and many others.

SECONDARY LIGHTING

In itself, primary lighting is inadequate for the specialized showing of merchandise. For this purpose, secondary lighting should be added: spot and flood lights to augment basic window lighting, to brighten the shelves, the cases, the counters and the merchandise so the customer's eye is attracted.

In this second phase of store illumination, lighting begins to function as a definite sales force. Even dresses hanging in stock areas or aprons on a counter become more appealing to the customer when illuminated. Besides selling the store, lighting is now selling the contents of the store. Secondary store illumination includes down-lighting from the ceiling, showcase lighting, and valance lighting.

Down-lighting is effective for illuminating merchandise on top of counters or inside glass cases. The light comes in a direct shaft from the ceiling or from an area above the counter. The lighting fixture should be placed at a point toward the customer's edge of the counter to avoid bright reflections from glass and shiny counter tops which will annoy the shopper.

Showcase lighting helps to overcome the glare created by reflections from the glass tops and the sliding doors of store furnishings. Showcase lighting used in an area above normal eye level must be carefully hidden. (See *Figure 25*.)

Valance lighting provides downward light for merchandise on shelves and in wall cases. Such lighting is easily hidden. Besides highlighting the merchandise on shelves and in wall cases, valance lighting may be directed upward to silhouette signs, to illuminate upper walls and to create a generally pleasant atmosphere.

This second phase of the store lighting pattern aids the customer in judging and comparing merchandise and in making the best choice of merchandise to meet his needs. Secondary lighting also assists the clerk in his effort to find what the customer wants quickly and efficiently.

Most display men prefer fluorescent tubes for use in secondary lighting situations because of their cool efficiency in close, and closed, areas and their soft, diffused light. Fluorescent tubes do not become overheated or cause fire hazards as quickly as incandescent bulbs. They give more light at a lower wattage, so that overloading of electric lines is avoided; and they spread their light over a wider area so as not to create a "spotty" lighting pattern which is often apparent when incandescent bulbs are used.

ATMOSPHERE LIGHTING

The final element in the store lighting pattern is atmosphere lighting. This is the phase that plays light against shadow to create the distinctive effect in specific displays. Highlight (the brightest spot of light on an object) is not directed on the merchandise only; it may be directed on a wall (as on glitter behind a fur coat display to give the illusion of coldness), on a mannequin or on a card containing copy about the merchandise. It is atmosphere lighting which concerns the display man most directly.

In the windows, color filters, pin-point spot lights and black lighting may be used to create dramatic effects. Inside the store, atmosphere lighting is used in featured displays. Take for example a furniture department where hassocks are standing about according to style and color. When one of these hassocks is singled out to be placed in a display area along with associated items, this featured display needs added lighting.

Atmosphere lighting concentrates more light on an area than either primary or secondary lighting provide. Since illumination for featured displays should be double the brightness of primary or secondary illumination, incandescent spotlights and floodlights are most often used. Spotlights concentrate light on a given spot or place. Floodlights cause the concentrated light to flare out or spread, and thus to flood the area.

DISPLAY ILLUMINATION

In achieving dramatic effects for a display area through atmosphere lighting, two distinct conditions present themselves to the display man: 1) light and shadow, and 2) color. Since light has as its natural source the sun which shines from above, or the side, display technicians use this knowledge in supplying atmosphere light to merchandise. Overhead lighting, or side lighting, is more adaptable for store displays than the foot-lighting found in theaters. One reason for this is the use of display fixtures: light coming from below a balsa board to which a sweater is pinned would shadow the merchandise and highlight the fixture. In this connection it is wise to mention that side or wing lighting is especially adaptable to furniture displays.

The play of light against shadow is one condition in the art of lighting merchandise. The light aimed at the nose of a mannequin causes a shadow on the cheek and neck; the light focused on the outside of a shoe causes a shadow to fall on the inside of the shoe. By playing light against shadow, emphasis is focused on the merchandise and the setting. It brings out the background, the accessories; it may emphasize any particular detail, but it must be used with finesse so as not to clutter the display with too much light or too many shadows and thus destroy its creative purpose.

The use of color to create a dramatic effect is another condition of atmosphere lighting. Colored lighting imitates the glow of moonlight or the warmth of sunlight; with its delicate shades it enchants unconsciously. Colored lights affect the passer-by's desires and are an inanimate expression of excitement and drama which appeals to the vanity of the customer.

Some light bulbs are made with color fused into the bulb-end, but these are not too satisfactory because the color is seldom intense enough. The use of color filters is the surest method for the display man to obtain colored lighting effects on a merchandise setting. Filters are more economical since they can be clamped on any bulb. They tone the illumination before it reaches the merchandise. Another type of color filter, the gelatin, may be used with special fixtures.

Filters are available in four colors—red, blue, green and amber—and they may be used in any number of effective combinations. The general suggestions which follow concern color filters:

Blue filters are valuable in creating sacred effects or night setting for merchandise. Blue on white makes white appear whiter.

Amber light is dramatic for background areas. It does not flatter merchandise too well, but it is excellent for tropical scenes.

Green light is seldom used on merchandise and is employed mainly for contrast or mysterious effects.

Red is never used directly on merchandise, and when the red tones are included in a display picture, they are used sparingly.

LIGHTING CHECKPOINTS

In all lighting for a store and its merchandise, the display man must always keep in mind the three "stop, look and listen" elements of illumination. These problems are *glare*, *merchandise* and *air circulation*. They can become quite involved at times and they should never be overlooked.

Glare: Any light which glares or shines in the eyes of the customer will blind him and thus repel patronage rather than inviting it. Window lighting techniques seldom have this problem to contend with because their lights are usually all aimed away from the street or well hidden by valances and wing partitions. Inside the store, however, the display man is confronted in each new display with the problem of light shining in a mirror or on glass, or a light angled improperly. In the place-

ment of spotlights, he projects the light downward at never more than a 45-degree angle. If there is still offensive glare at this angle, filters and louvers may be attached to the bulb end of the lighting fixture to channel the beam of light.

Merchandise itself poses a two-fold problem in store illumination. First, there is the need for showing merchandise to the customer as it actually is so that he will know exactly what he is buying. Very often customers will demand that worsteds be taken outside the store or to a nearby window to observe their coloring in pure daylight. The customer does not want merchandise which appears dramatic in the store but changes completely when he sees it for the first time at home. Consequently, daylight tones of lighting are the nearest semblance for sunlight and the bright outdoors. Daylight tones glamorize the merchandise but do not change the apparent quality or real color of the items displayed. Most display areas are, therefore, illuminated with the filament type incandescent spotlight or floodlight. Fluorescent lighting is modern, cheaper and cooler, but it does change the true color and brilliance of some merchandise. Jewelry departments use incandescent light exclusively for this reason. Secondly, merchandise left under a strong light for too long a time will become dingy in appearance. High wattage illumination fades merchandise to a certain extent. Blue merchandise is especially susceptible to this fading process and must be watched carefully if used in any display.

Heat and air circulation comprise the third problem of display illumination. *Fluorescent* lighting is cool and issues forth from long tubes lined with a fluorescent powder. This type of lighting creates very little heat. *Incandescent* lighting, the bulb and filament type of illumination, produces quite a bit of heat. In a small area, this concentrated heat may become a fire hazard. When using incandescent spot or flood lights in display areas, the display man remembers to maintain ample space for air circulation, installs the bulbs away from sprinkler heads, and directs their rays away from inflammable objects.

The importance of light in a display cannot be too much emphasized. Proper lighting throughout a store acts as a magnet upon the customer's senses; it immediately invites him to draw closer and inspect the merchandise. Because store illumination is such a dominant force in selling, the display man is constantly on the alert for changing techniques to improve the lighting in his windows, his departments and his settings.

Part II

THE *WHY* OF DISPLAY

6 Importance of Display

Every retailing establishment is in business for one reason—to ring the cash register with a sale. The success of any store lies in its ability to sell, sell, SELL. And, strangely enough, the problem of selling is not always confined to dollars and cents. As well as selling merchandise, a store must sell an idea of good will to the customer each time he enters the store. Having sold this idea thoroughly, there is no question in the customer's mind about returning to the store again and again, and very soon.

THE FAVORITE STORE

Just why does an individual go into one store rather than another? Why single out one of the many masonry edifices along a street for his favorite store? In every town, every city across the nation, there is always one store that seems to surpass the other in popularity. Of all the corner drug stores there will be one which is thought of first, perhaps because of its specialty in sundries. Of all the laundries in town there will be one which is considered best because of its perfect finish on shirts or its attention to minor details of repair. Of all the bakeries in town there will be one, surely, which makes delicious eclairs, *mais oui*. One particular bank will take a personalized interest in each account. Of all the men's shops in a town, one will be patronized for its adeptness in dressing its customers.

Chicagoans call their favorite store "Fields." Dallas is famous for its Neiman-Marcus; Miami has its Burdine's and New Yorkers are justly proud of Lord & Taylor and "Macy's." In Los Angeles there is The May Company; in Seattle it is Bon Marche. Atlanta has its Rich's, and in New Orleans it is Maison Blanche. Scattered in towns and hamlets throughout America are Sear's, Penney's and Rexall chain stores. Each has a characteristic of its own. An establishment does not necessarily have to be huge in acreage or elite in its board of directors to become a favorite with its customers. There are shoeshine boys who have regular patrons because of an engaging grin; a sidewalk newsstand that is *the* place to get what is desired in newsprint because of its wide selection of out-of-town newspapers.

What motivates this consistent show of favoritism on the part of customers? What particularly influences the selection? Mainly, a customer chooses one store over another store for one of five reasons, its *merchandise, advertising, service, position* or *display*.

Merchandise makes a store different from stores across the street. One looks for a hardware store when one wants a nail. Visiting hardware stores from state to state, you find the merchandise carried in each of them is very much alike. The alikeness would not extend to the entire stock, or the entire range of sizes, or assortment of goods; however, the merchandise would be of a basically similar character. A hardware store in Minneapolis would sell the same brand of nails as would be found in a hardware store in St. Louis. A person would not enter a bakery to purchase a nail, but most bakeries sell pastries and nails may be found in hardware stores. Therefore, merchandise unconsciously influences the selection of a store.

Advertising is another influence which determines whether a customer will patronize a certain store. Advertising policy and layout fall into rather general types. Most jewelry store advertisements are similar in make-up; furniture stores tend to feature certain items in a preconceived cycle; chain stores and discount houses follow set policies often laid down by their home offices. Consequently, a men's store advertisement for Father's Day ties will be quite similar in Maine and Montana, in Texas and Tennessee. The advertisement will influence the reader's choice of store by the prices offered or the merchandise shown in the newspaper.

Service tends also to differentiate a store from other stores. The most valuable special service any business establishment can offer is a friendly, helpful clerk. Nearly every store prides itself upon being able to say: "In our store, the customer is always right." One store may offer free postage on out-of-town packages; another may have faster elevators or newer escalators, while a third furnishes personalized bridal service to a young lady purchasing such apparel there.

Position and prestige, or store image as it is sometimes called, affect an individual's impulse to become a steady customer. If the individual purchases a gift for a very special relative, he naturally desires to make a good impression. He, therefore, chooses a store of social standing equal to his relative. Having made the purchase, he finds the store is not so coldly elegant as he had supposed and that the prices are not any higher than those in less prestige-minded shops. He comes back again and again because of the added prestige he feels in relation to the store. A customer chooses the store with a building and fixtures that have kept pace with modern design. Prestige stores occasionally maintain that the customer is not always right and seek to show him why this is so; they sponsor new and daring fashions and keep the individual aware of controversial merchandise in a friendly manner.

Display, however, combines all these factors in helping a customer choose a store for his preference because all that any store has to offer the customer is shown in a unique way. The special services and the merchandise advertised to the customer for selection are presented through display on the premises in the windows and the interior. A full page advertisement may have told the customer of handbags which a store suggests as gifts. How disappointing to come into the store and find only the bags on a counter with a sign reading "As Advertised." The customer may have heard that the store has a check room for excess parcels, but it may take him quite awhile to locate it if there are no signs to direct him. When shopping, a customer wants to have his desires anticipated. In window and interior displays the character and the policy and the friendliness and the merchandise of a store are clearly demonstrated.

Window display will halt the individual and invite him to turn in at the front door. But good display does not end at the nearest entrance. The interior of the store must continue the impression that the front windows and advertising have created. There is no worse disappointment to the esthetic nature of a customer than to come from strikingly chic street windows into drab, uninspired main floor interiors. Interior display begins at the front door and invites the passer-by at every turn, with each step, to become a regular and contented customer.

No matter how good a product is, it will not sell unless presented properly, dramatically, and in a way which inspires the individual to buy. In this aspect, display is even competing successfully with advertising.

Display is so important in retailing today because it gives character to inanimate objects for sale by placing them in a dramatic, life-like situation. Good display integrates salable items with everyday living and everyday needs. To the display artist, a shoe is not only a shoe of size six made of leather and laced or buckled. Properly displayed, the shoe appears to be stepping on an escalator, on an accelerator, crushing out a cigarette, walking down the aisle at graduation, dancing until two in the morning, holding a croquet ball in place to send a rival's ball away with a mallet close at hand, or simply lying beside a golf ball in such a manner as to show the cleated sole.

Sometimes the dramatic part played by display is so great that the customer will demand to buy what is displayed rather than an identical article from stock. "It didn't look like that one," he will say firmly. And it did not: the dramatic presentation is missing. The shoe on display seemed alive and charming; the shoe in the box is stiff and less alluring.

DISPLAY COORDINATION

Lovely merchandise pictures do not happen by chance. They are planned, discussed, criticized and

Saks 34th Street, New York

Stern's, New York

26 SPECIAL PROMOTIONS

consciously directed to aid the clerk in selling more merchandise, to improve the appearance of the store as a whole and to please the customer at every turn. Display is not a potpourri of color, flowers, paper and merchandise. Impressive settings are brought about by long-range planning, earnest labor and a flair for concocting merchandise pictures just a little differently from any other display.

Coordination in display is needed so that the store will not become four or five stores in one, but rather will present a simple continuous theme throughout its windows and departments. It is poor technique to be accentuating a sale in one department while featuring vacation fashions in another and home furnishings specials in the windows. Each year, a time should be designated well in advance for the sale, the home furnishings promotion and the vacation specials, and then the entire store should be given over to campaigning for that special event. If there is to be a sale upstairs, there should be a sale downstairs and in the windows, too. (See *Figure 26.*) True, a home furnishings promotion will consist of furniture, rugs and draperies; but linens may be coordinated with these items also. Suggesting a new garbage pail, special cleaning aids or a book which explains how to make slip covers, will tie in other departments with the promotion. Certainly a mannequin dressed in the latest fashion may be placed in the bedroom display, and a doll from the toy department on the bed would suggest a child's world of home furnishings.

Through coordination of theme in all departments of a store, order comes out of chaos and the customer is not asked at every turn to change his thinking pattern. Also, through suggestive display of related items, the sales figures in all departments improve.

Neiman-Marcus, that fabulous store in Texas, proves beyond a doubt the success of displays which are coordinated throughout a store. Not so many years ago, at Christmastime, this store used white ostrich plumes for its complete interior decor. White ostrich trees, white ostrich garlands and chandeliers covered with white ostrich plumes made the store a breathtaking sight. No person entering the store could go away without remarking about its beauty. What a setting for any merchandise!

Again, as a spring promotion, Neiman-Marcus completely coordinated displays of merchandise with carnations—thousands of real blossoms. A full-sized willow tree drooping with myriads of real carnations was used in the center aisle of the main floor. Ledges were edged with carnation hedges; mannequins were even fashioned from carnations. The stairways leading upward were surrounded with dried cactus plants festooned with these carnations. The stationery department featured scented papers and the beauty salon originated a "Carnation Cut" coiffure. Besides heralding spring and Mother's Day, this galaxy of carnations was used at Neiman-Marcus to promote a new color in Elizabeth Arden cosmetics.

The Crescent, in Spokane, is another fine example of display that stresses a given theme. If The Crescent wants to present a color, that color really gets shown. If pink is the chosen color, everywhere the customer looks he is met with an illusion of pink. Every mannequin wears pink. There are pink lights, pink floors, pink backgrounds, pink flowers, pink hats, pink gloves. Nothing is haphazard at The Crescent; when they are in the pink, they are wholly in the pink.

Likewise, when Macy's of New York decides to put on a super colossal sale, no detail is forgotten. Huge clown heads dominate the windows; giant eight foot clowns guard the ledges; aerial trapeze artists are suspended from the ceiling; bright sale posters carry through the theme, sign toppers call attention to the merchandise and gay bunting gives additional color to the carnival interior.

One season the L. T. Samuel's women's apparel store of Ogden, Utah, presented a completely coordinated theme—Spring in Japan. Merchandise was charmingly presented in a way which seemed effortless to the customer but which had entailed extensive planning on the part of the display staff. Many of the props used with the merchandise were actual imports from Japan, and each of the ten windows was designed around a single color scheme. Hand-painted lanterns and cloth screens, silk parasols, bright sketches, clear photographs and oriental lettering on the window cards added to the authentic atmosphere. The Japanese theme was carried over into the store. Colored silk print dresses, appropriately accessorized, predominated in the display areas; caged canaries were used as an accent in the various departments.

Display themes for merchandise presentations do not spring full-grown like Minerva from Zeus' head. Themes require research and constant planning if they are to succeed in bringing the customer back again and again.

Many stores hesitate to experiment with a coordinated display effort. They have heard of its use; they have seen the conclusive proof of increased sales resulting from such merchandising techniques; yet they hesitate to avail themselves of the added profit involved in the use of these techniques. By their reticence, they shun a chance to become the preferred store in their city, town, hamlet or shopping center.

If big stores believe in all-encompassing display, the smaller store should follow their examples on a smaller scale. If the larger stores have proven the worth of display, more display, better display; smaller stores should at least give display techniques a fair trial before dismissing their importance with a shrug of the shoulders and the remark "It costs too much!" The sooner retailers bring display into their store and into their budgets, the sooner they will begin to realize the profit and prestige of being one of the favorite stores in the community.

Synonymous with coordination in display is the need for cooperation from clerks, buyers and managers. If the display man has to beg and plead, returning again and again to a certain department for necessary information, the process of showing merchandise is impeded. Also, dispositions become strained and inspiration is often hampered. On the other hand, if merchandise and information are ready and waiting and have been planned far in advance by the buyers, the showing and selling of merchandise becomes a pleasant task. When each department manager, each buyer and each clerk has been made aware of the help which dramatic displays will give them—in increased sales, lower inventories and higher prestige—they will join the surge toward more and better displays.

7 Psychological Aspects

While the main objective of retailing establishments is to sell merchandise and thus serve the individual, the true motive for all buying is to satisfy certain needs or desires inherent in everyday life. The individual goes shopping with very serious needs in mind: junior needs shoes or the faucet needs a new washer or the lamp in the living room needs another shade. But the shopper coming into a store, being human, has conscious as well as subconscious desires: perhaps the wish for a smaller waistline, perhaps a longing to be more attractive, possibly the impulse to dare just once to be frivolous and taste of luxury.

THE SERIOUS SHOPPER

The prospective customer with a preconceived idea of just exactly what and how much he is going to buy is termed the serious shopper. He has a list which he checks off as he buys the items noted there. If he needs a pair of scissors, he shops several stores, looking at the types of scissors available and comparing their prices—then he buys the scissors. Having made purchase number one on his list, he proceeds to the second and the third purchase, and so on. Usually the serious shopper buys only what he came into the store to purchase and immediately leaves the premises. Very often, however, the serious shopper may become an impulse shopper too. Display areas throughout a store invite the serious shopper to become an impulse shopper and purchase some item not on his list.

To think of merchandise other than that on his list, the serious shopper must have his attention diverted and held. Curiosity must be aroused in his mind to see more of the item which he has just passed. Here, display really seeks to awaken the customer's subconscious desires.

Perhaps a sports shirt has been placed so that a sleeve is apparently casting with rod and reel. The background may be a tree beside a brook. By the shirt is a rugged pair of brogues and above the collar of the sports shirt has been placed a cap with visor. The merchandise is dramatized so as to attain an effect of very real conditions and thus reinforce the customer's need and desire for the merchandise.

Suppose the serious shopper came into the store with a sports shirt on his list. The work of the display man suggested to him that the shoes, cap and fishing gear are indispensable to the wearer's enjoyment of that shirt. Display thus fostered the impulse to buy more than the shirt. The serious shopper, with the sport shirt on his list, added the shoes and cap to his purchases and became an impulse shopper, too. He was caught up in the drama of display.

THE IMPORTANT WOMAN

The shopper has repeatedly been referred to here as *he*. This has been done only as the preferred grammatical term. In retailing, in the merchandising field, the customer is usually a *she*. Well over three-fourths of all purchases made today in the United States are made by women. *She* buys the children's clothes. *She* decorates the home. *She* shops for groceries. *She* chooses the linens. *She* wants the garden planted. *She* prepares for the vacation. And *he* pays for most of it. A. E. Hurst, in *Selling Merchandise for Profit*, reported a New York survey which was conducted in twelve classes of retail stores as to the purchases made by men and women with the following results:

Type of Store or Merchandise	Per Cent of Purchases By Men	By Women
Drug Store	23%	77%
Department Store	18	82
Grocery Store	19	81
Silks	2	98
Pianos	22	78
Leather Goods	33	67
Automobiles	59	41
Hardware	51	49
Electric Supplies	20	80
Jewelry	25	75
Men's Socks	20	80
Men's Neckwear	37	63

Men enjoy buying motors, guns, fishing tackle, large appliances, television sets, houses, cars, tools and office equipment. They renege at trivial purchases such as a graduation gift for nephew John, a wedding present for friends Anthony and Susan, or sheets for the bed and moth preventives for the closet. A man's wife or his sister or his mother does these shopping chores. The male is too occupied making money, building the homes and running the businesses of America to bother with everyday buying.

Knowing that the shoppers of today are more often women than men, retailers appeal to the feminine flair for luxury, beauty and romance. A ship made of puffy lace sails with a pipe for a rudder will entice the female. Not so the man; for him the ship must be seaworthy. Men demand a practical approach to display; for a woman, the effectiveness of a display is often augmented by a touch of the frivolous.

Whether the customer be *he* or *she*, a serious shopper with a list, a passer-by with no particular intention of buying or a person merely waiting to meet another person in the store, the importance of proper display techniques and their influence upon the customer cannot be over emphasized.

SURVEY RESULTS

If reported success in the use of display theories will not persuade the store owner as to a need for better, expanded usage, perhaps some cold, hard percentages will. The survey results which follow are based on facts, not upon preconceived ideas; therefore, their conclusions must be accepted.

A Cluett, Peabody Survey was made of sales resulting from an ensembled display of related merchandise compared with the sales when that merchandise was shown alone and unrelated. Men's ties and handkerchiefs were shown on counters and tables in separate areas. On studying the buying habits of the customers, it was found that 4 to 9 percent of the tie buyers also bought handkerchiefs from another counter. Then the ties and handkerchiefs were displayed together on the same counter—a matching handkerchief for each tie. When the two items were shown together, 57 percent of the tie buyers also bought handkerchiefs.

Another study considered ties and shirts shown separately and together. Only 2 out of 10 shirt buyers bought ties when the merchandise was segregated in different areas. However, when the ties and shirts were shown together and related, 7 out of 10 shirt buyers purchased ties.

A Display Research Survey presented several pairs of men's shoes placed casually on a counter area, and the behavior of the traffic exposed to the display was observed. It was found that 32 percent of the passers-by looked at the display and 35 percent of these lookers prolonged their interest to a definite stop at the display, thus giving the salesperson near the counter an opportunity to speak to a number of customers.

A second type of display was substituted for the first one, and customer behavior was studied. The second display employed only the shoe for the right foot shown under a hanging, creased trouser cuff of appropriate worsted. Of the customer traffic exposed to the second display, 37 percent looked—the display reached 5 percent more of the people exposed—and 44 percent of the lookers prolonged their interest by stopping at the display. With the use of an associative piece of merchandise, the salesperson was afforded 9 percent more opportunity to approach the customer.

Traffic response to a window display was studied in another survey at one of the Broadway windows of Macy's, New York. The window was first curtained off, and the behavior of pedestrians was noted. For easier comparison, the sample size was set at 100,000. In this survey, 70,000 women and 30,000 men passed the designated, curtained window; 1,300–1,600 women and 700 men actually looked at the window when passing it.

Then an appropriate display of merchandise was installed and the window was opened to view.

Now 39,000 of the 70,000 women who passed looked at the window, and 8,400 of the 30,000 men passing glanced at the window display. By drawing the curtain and exposing the passer-by to attractively placed merchandise, it was demonstrated that 7,800 additional men and 38,000 additional women became aware of merchandise offered for sale.

A visual merchandising research report studied the total number of sales of given items in three distinct counter situations. Each area was first considered with the merchandise shown flat or in a disorderly fashion. Then arrangement of the merchandise was altered and a display setting was introduced.

1. The original display of jewelry boxes sold a total of 27 percent of the items during a test period. Revised display techniques sold 73 percent of the total items offered during a test period.
2. A revised display of cake pans showed an increase in sales of 18 percent.
3. A revised display of razor blade disposal pieces showed an increase of 74 percent in units sold.

A Gilbert Youth survey studied the buying habits of boys and girls throughout America, comparing their potentialities and influences upon the spending quotas of the American family. These researchers found that over 50 percent of the youth market—ages 8 to 20 years—earn extra money of their own by part-time work.

It was found that the age group of 11 to 20 exerts a tremendous influence on family buying. Forty-eight percent of the girls shop entirely by themselves and make their own selections. Sixty-four percent of the boys from ages 13 to 15 said their idea of what to wear came from what others wear; 30 percent got their ideas from magazines; 22 percent from the recommendations of their favorite store; and 14 percent from the movies. (Total equals more than 100 percent due to multiple sources of ideas.)

The researchers found that fashion shows, milk or coke bars and special promotions tend to increase sales in youth markets and make these age groups feel at home in their departments of a store. Correlated displays yield more business in these departments.

These surveys and studies concretely prove that when display techniques are employed realistically in the small store as well as the large urban or suburban selling center, sales figures show a marked upward swing.

8 Dramatic Setting Is Important

Relating merchandise to human needs and activities is the secret of good visual merchandising and the mainspring of all display themes. The power of suggestion is enormous in selling, and methods for making merchandise come alive constitute the creative part of display. The manner in which goods are presented to the customer invariably determines the sale. The selling power of display will be influenced by the association used, *i.e.*, how attractively the stage is set for the merchandise.

The ability to associate ideas with merchandise in proper sequence is not attained without forethought and work. The alert display man is always just one step ahead of the customer. He knows that the woman who has to economize during her early married years finds it easier to acquire more expensive things as her husband's resources expand. He knows that the young working girl, who three years ago was looked after by her parents, is now making her own selections of everything on a much more meager budget. He knows that he must introduce the new, the startling, by associating it with the old and tried experience of the customer.

SELL WHAT IT CAN DO

In his effort to interest a customer in merchandise within a store, the display man begins to think less and less of the merchandise itself—as inanimate objects—and concentrates upon what the merchandise can do, where it can go with the customer and how it is made, thereby forming animate situations. He uses tasteful backgrounds and accessories to suggest how the merchandise may benefit the customer.

The modern display man does not sell wearing apparel alone; he dramatizes the clothes in such a way that he sells the neat and polished appearance along with the plaids and the nylons. He sells shoes by suggesting foot comfort and style; books by hinting at the lasting benefits of knowledge or the pleasant passing of a leisure hour. He sells automobile tires by suggesting their low cost and long wearing quality or the blow-out protection they afford; tractors or plows by reminding the customer of the beautiful fields of wheat or corn that plows and tractors will cultivate. The display man never sells things; he sells ideas, feelings and happiness. When he has succeeded in doing this, he suddenly finds himself with no problems at all in the way of displaying his store's good will to the community.

SOURCES FOR IDEAS

In searching for creative ideas to help him present merchandise dramatically, his sources include *extensive reading in related fields, season and news, the known with the unknown, merchandise, throw-aways or raw materials, doodling or a change of pace,* and *special devices.*

Extensive reading in relation to ideas means that the display person scans everything he can find concerning the many aspects of his field.

Along with the local newspapers he should read *Woman's Wear Daily*. Books, such as those included in the bibliography (Appendix v) help him evaluate his situation and cope with its problems. Current magazines like *Holiday, Life, Fortune, Modern Living, Better Homes and Gardens*, etc., offer endless display ideas.

Fashion magazines—*Vogue, Glamour, Esquire, Harper's Bazaar* and *McCall's*—present coming trends and merchandise. Completely planned advertising promotions are a part of each issue of such publications, and these may easily be transposed to almost any display need.

Paul T. Knapp, writing in the March, 1963, issue of *Display World*, editoralizes this point:

"Retailing executives, publishers of major consumer publications and members of all sales promotion media will be watching closely for the results of a current experiment of McCall's, the world's largest magazine for women, and Macy's, department store chain with 41 stores throughout the U.S. including the largest department store in the world in New York City.

"The experiment is probably the largest and most comprehensive coordination of national magazine advertising and retail display every ventured and could well establish a pattern of in-depth sales promotion worth developing even farther.

"Briefly, here is how it works: Fifty-nine different national brand products were either advertised or mentioned editorially in the February McCall's and these items are carried by all Macy's stores, which include Bamberger's, New Jersey; Davison-Paxon Co., Georgia; LaSalle & Koch Co., Ohio; and Macy's, New York, California, Kansas and Missouri—41 in all.

"In-store promotion involved extensive point-of-purchase displays including counter cards, toppers to go with Macy's regular sign holders, as well as blow-ups of McCall's cover and 30 full-color pages. Of course, windows made excellent use of the editorial titles: 'Pink's the color in Spring Fashions,' 'New Again Kitchens,' 'Every Day in Every Way You're Getting Prettier and Prettier.'

"Further coordination was carried out in blue and lavender artwork on gift boxes, local newspaper advertising and, of course, posters for Grand Central and Pennsylvania Stations in New York City.

"We would like to applaud this promotional experiment and extend our congratulations even before it is announced as an astounding success."

Trade magazines, such as *Display World, Department Store Economist*, etc., often suggest solutions to problems which other stores throughout America are experiencing daily. They show what the "big" stores are doing; they suggest how the smaller store can do likewise; they help the retailer keep pace with the changing buying habits of his customer. They present surveys and reports on business in many states which may prove valuable to the display man.

Season and news are helpful in suggesting the use or need for merchandise and thereby presenting it dramatically. Springtime displays could feature baby chicks and a barnyard scene along with the merchandise. They might show a cock crowing over some special values for the customer. Easter merchandise pictures are always dressy and have a sacred feeling. Kites, maypoles, Father's Day, June brides, vacation time, back-to-school, campus life and Christmas are but a few of the seasonal connotations a display man may choose for his merchandise. Nature presents a crowded gallery of display pictures from which to choose. A leaf here in its proper time, a flower there when the season has changed—a glorious magnolia blossom in June, a saucy jonquil in March. That is the real world brought into the man-made world of the store. People are influenced by the season, the weather; and people are customers.

News items and local events will influence a store's display of merchandise. What is going on now in the community which might conceivably be used as a display setting? A circus is coming to town; there are concerts and plays; this is Fire Prevention Week, Girl Scout Week, Book Week. Institutional projects such as the charity drive, a subscription for a new hospital or an annual flower club activity deserve notice along with related merchandise in a store. The spring dance at a college will suggest perfect settings for the display man to show the debutante what his store has in evening shoes, gloves, lingerie, hosiery, a beautiful gown, a wrap and surely perfumes. A horse show, as a coming event, affords the alert display man a chance to show his "Blue Ribbon Winners"—merchandise appropriate for the occasion.

By associating the known with the unknown in retailing, the customer will not feel diffident about new types of merchandise. Introduce him to them with something familiar, with something he has already understood and experienced. The customer may be excited into action toward a color merely by the way it is presented. Consider the thought changes brought about in the mind with such prefixes to the word grey as slate, pewter, charcoal, dawn or battleship.

All our thoughts are habit grooved. Suggest a new type rug backing for safety by asking "Did you ever trip over a rug?" Feature a TV accessory with the inquiry "Does snow spoil your enjoyment of TV?"

Merchandise itself will often suggest an associative idea to use with that merchandise. The plaid lining of a jacket will naturally suggest bagpipes and Scottish dances; the name of a certain material might be exploited with background effects—Victorian chintz, French lace, camel's hair coats, Japanese prints. Italian hand-screened scarfs attached to an artist's easel with brush and pallet nearby will show graphically that they were done by hand; small pieces of Roman statuary in the background can add to the artistic flavor of the display. Leather handbags no longer present a merely inanimate picture when they are displayed against a background mural of the tanning processes, alligator farms or ranch scenes. Silver pieces gain immeasurably in elegance and interest when displayed along with authentic notations on their history, tracing their lineage back to medieval and court ceremonies, or when shown in a setting to promote the various uses one piece of silver may have.

Of course, each age group reacts differently to these notations in a display. The child loves gaudy, bright things; the adult enjoys frivolity, romance, daring situations; the aging individual always compares the things of today with "When I was a boy . . ." In presenting a merchandise picture to suggest vacation needs and camping fun, hot dogs or soda pop antics interest the growing child; fishing tackle, resort clothes and sun tan lotion appeal to the adult; while a good book, a device to keep the mosquitos away, or a suggestion of complete relaxation mean more to the aging customer. The display man applies all this knowledge to the particular situation at hand.

Throw aways or raw materials used along with merchandise to be displayed save time and money for the display man. Lace paper doilies, crepe paper, bricks, old shutters or even coat hangers may be used for added appeal in merchandise pictures.

On a vacation at the seashore, the display man does not overlook some piece of driftwood he might find. He brings home a bag of shells gathered or a bucket of the beautiful white sand which can seldom be purchased locally.

If a family reunion will be held at the farm soon, he doesn't forget to browse the barn and its rafters for old buggy wheels, some used peck baskets, or even a battered milking stool or can. These make delightful display props after a little spit and polish has been applied.

And an alert display person never overlooks the yellow pages of the telephone directory for a latch-on-to idea that is different. Quail raised in captivity are a novelty. How many children have never seen the familiar bobwhite songster close at hand? Or he has some fan-tailed pigeons dyed in

colors to match a promotion and allows them to strut about caged near a display.

Here too, the many foliages on the market for display uses—natural, preserved, paper, cloth, gaudy, sophisticated, photographic—should be remembered. A myriad array of bird cages, commercial murals, mannequins and props of every description are always accessible to the artist seeking to present attractive merchandise pictures.

Doodling or a change of pace is important to the display man for he strives constantly to use the old in a different way. He uses hearts at Valentine's Day, but not red ones; bunnies at Easter, but idealistic ones; palm trees in mid winter, or a chess board with merchandise on the squares instead of chess pieces.

Change of pace is very necessary in dynamic display. A shift in the type of setting used in any department will catch the customer by surprise and cause him to look forward to seeing what additional changes have been made since his last visit to the store. After featuring windows given over entirely to color themes—a Skipper Blue window, a Dynamite Red window, an Urban Black window—it is wise to themize the windows differently by placing emphasis on situations such as Honeymoon Secrets, Cherished Memories, Fun for All the Family, or Mother's Little Helper.

Having employed no-seam papers of pastel tints in cases for several months, the display man interests his customer with florals or bold striped papers. Just as surprise endings are sometimes used in writing novels and plays, so the unusual things in display are pleasing to the customer.

Quite often the setting of an interior display will be timely and usable for a month, as a June bride promotion, or even a whole season, as a fall back-to-school promotion, and may therefore be freshened up simply with a dusting and adjustment here and there. This does not mean that the merchandise should not be changed. Merchandise definitely should be changed in display areas every seven to fourteen days because:

1. The same people often pass a display area daily and they like to see new or different displays.

2. Periodic changes assure better coordination between departments and emphasize the promotion of merchandise.

3. The customer will become acquainted with more of the varied stock a store has to offer.

4. Items left on display too long soil, fade, rust, become dingy and therefore cannot be sold as first quality merchandise.

5. Displays are the most conspicuous part of the store, and they should be kept interesting at all times.

A change of pace relieves the monotony of display upon display, stack upon stack of items, and may mean the difference between merchandise merely shown and merchandise definitely seen and sold.

Special devices used in display include motion, sound and dispensing.

Motion in display surprises the passer-by and immediately attracts him. The conveyor belt kind of motion which presents a panorama of still life passing by a given spot is most intriguing to youngsters. Dolls, tin soldiers, Santa's helpers gaily at work and other merchandise itself may be used in motion for display. Hidden electric fans add liveliness to merchandise pictures, *i.e.*, a fan might be blowing pennants telling of a sale to come in the store. A pointing finger or even a turntable will add appeal to merchandise. What customer is not attracted by the panorama of an electric train rolling along a miniature country-side?

Very often motion is suggested without the actual use of devices. Motion may be implied by an illusion of liquid flowing from a bottle, by a toy airplane hung from the ceiling or by a manne-quin suspended in mid air. Turntables are most helpful in showing merchandise from all angles. A complete view of the merchandise is thereby gained, not just its front, side or back. Some turn-tables are so small as to hold only a fountain pen while others are massive enough to support a single mannequin or an entire room setting. Turntables maintain stationary motion within an area and seldom detract from the rest of the setting.

Broadcasting *sound* from the windows or ex-terior of the building is prohibited in many cities. Under such restrictions, if bells are shown ringing in the window the sound that would normally peal forth must be imagined by the passer-by. Such noises as Santa chuckling when he pops down a chimney or soft religious music are often permitted on special occasions. Sounds used for display purposes inside the store, however, have only to outvoice the hubbub of customer-clerk talk and other noises, and are therefore usually confined to small areas because the volume of their sound would prohibit use over a large area. Demonstrators often use sound equipment; ex-hibits and fashion shows are commented upon over loud speaker systems; semi-classical music may be played softly in specialty shops.

Another device used for appeal in display is *dispensing*. Dispensing is a term which includes all efforts to sell merchandise which allow the customer to touch, taste or smell the item. It includes the giving away of free samples, the use of fountains bubbling with cologne to spread a cosmetic essence, and the employment of special demonstrators to show why a product is useful.

Again and again the display man discovers in his search for appealing display ideas that he seldom uses an idea exactly as he saw it or read about it. He considers his own setting, his mer-chandise and his customer in relation to the original suggestion. He tempers the idea to comply with his store policy and the immediate needs of a department. Ideas that are right for New York may be too urban for shoppers in a small town; promotions that were a success in Chicago may not be interesting to customers in a southern city. Ideas, however, are of paramount importance to display.

With any idea or setting, it is important that the merchandise dominate. The background, the setting, should enhance the merchandise and yet never overshadow it. The foliage used to suggest an autumn season is not for sale; the ranch scene behind the handbags is not there to suggest that the store is a travel bureau. The circus decor of a window is not meant to sell the confetti or the clowns or the masks; it is intended to interest the customer in the merchandise displayed.

True, the setting may stop the customer and invite him to see the merchandise at closer range, but having done that it should fade away in the mind of the customer and the merchandise should remain dominant. Huge window areas have been used to display one dress, one chair or one man's tie, and yet the setting around them was only a feeling, a suggestion. Quite often the very sim-plicity or neatness of a display will attract and interest the customer. The wise display man uses discretion and finesse when seeking dramatic ideas.

9   The Lost Causes

Just as the Indian tribes of America are many times referred to as the lost race, so display has its lost cause. Every year many of the religious sects of America have what they term a Revival—a renewing of effort to reaffirm basic principles and invite others to join their cause. Display, as a profession, needs more of this revival interest on the part of its workers. In its surge forward to take its place in the retailing professions, display has bypassed four very important counterparts: *the small store, men's wear departments, mass merchandise* and *copy*. These have become the lost causes of visual merchandising techniques.

Not that these four lost causes are not progressing—indeed they are; not that they are not trying—assuredly they do; not that they are not needed—most definitely they are. It is just that they have been unduly neglected and shunned. They have been overshadowed by the "big" store and its high pressure salesmanship. In a way, these four lost causes of display have allowed themselves to be neglected because they have been willing to drift along in a pattern that was set years and years ago. They must be awakened to the endless help modern display techniques can give; they must not remain lackadaisical if they hope to keep pace with modern retailing.

THE SMALL STORE

The first and most important lost cause of display is the small store. When visiting the shopping centers of any hamlet or town in America, it is usually difficult to tell where one plate glass window ends and the next begins. Inside, the pot-bellied stove of general store days is usually gone and there are electric lights, but fixtures do not seem sparkling and clean. The premises have been painted in the last two years, but there are unsightly mop splashings along the wall. Most store fronts are modern and rather well kept, but it has been a month or more since the glass was last polished spotlessly inside as well as outside, and the merchandise placed there looks rather shoddy. Where is the initiative, the push, the competitive urge to make the small store the most important in all the town?

Perhaps the merchandise in the small store is up-to-date, but too often it is piled haphazardly on tables or stacked halfway to the ceiling in boxes which are broken and dirty. Perhaps the fixtures and furnishings show the merchandise for the customer, but they haven't been moved, or angled, or changed in any way for years.

One of the most common delusions among small store owners is the idea that they have to spend a great deal of money before they can go in for display of any sort. Certain conventional display materials are helpful to begin with, but it doesn't always require a vast investment to improve displays. Money helps, but initiative and hard work can often overcome a lack of funds.

Each week, each month, rural inhabitants make a trek to the "big city" to buy. They travel miles to touch the glamour the "big city" has to offer. Much of that glamour, that drama, that newness,

71

could be brought right to them at home. Actually, small stores are always able to approximate big store methods on a small store scale. The small store has an excellent chance of surpassing the big store, in fact, because of its closer association with the employee, the community and the customer. The small store will no longer be a lost cause when it is able to conquer the feeling of insecurity which insists that it put a sample of its entire stock in the window.

A small store becomes a big store when it begins to act like one. This is not always a question of dollar volume. When a store begins to plan, when a store starts setting goals for itself and its clerks, when it keeps itself under control yet expands its resources and service, when a store avails itself of the extensive benefits of better display and advertising methods, when it becomes customer conscious, then the small store is becoming a big one. When a store is operated by three or four people at most, the problems of buying and selling become so demanding that the prestige factors of merchandising are often overlooked completely and put off until another day. Soon that day becomes weeks, months, years away and the store remains one among the many up and down the street.

The strength of the small store lies in its adherence to the two principles that first brought department stores into being about a hundred years ago—service and promotion. Not just adequate service but beyond-the-call-of-duty service; not cute and clever promotion so much as the sort that subtly burrows into the shoppers' minds to saturate them with confidence and loyalty.

People are beginning to migrate away from the hot, cramped, bustling hubbub of metropolitan areas. The trend is toward the suburban, and that is a trend in the direction of the small store.

Let it be emphasized here, however, that there are many small stores up and down the main streets of America which do a neat, inspiring job of display day-in and day-out. The staggering fact that they change the merchandise in their windows every week, every month—some of them every day—deserves a congratulatory note.

In a world of retailing giants like Macy's, Marshall Fields, The May Company and Nieman-Marcus, the smaller department stores often go unnoticed. This is unfortunate because, although small by comparison, many of them could teach these giants much in the way of courtesy and values.

Among the hundreds of small-city, sleepy-village retail operations in America today which do an outstanding job are stores like Bresee's of Oneonta, New York; Hess's in Allentown, Pennsylvania; and the Morris Store in Metuchen, New Jersey.

They are the champions of a seemingly lost cause in display.

MEN'S WEAR DEPARTMENTS

A second lost cause in display techniques is men's wear, particularly men's apparel stores. Many haberdasheries appear today almost as they did in the twenties. Merchandise has kept pace with the years. Knee britches, brightly colored shirt sleeve bands and detachable collars have given way to casual denim ensembles and open-collared, puckered nylon sports shirts, or the "his" and "her" combination. But the shirt display is still shirts in a row and the trouser display is still a window full of slacks.

These men's apparel displays are as alike as toy soldiers in a row. They seem to be planned on the assumption that a man need only look, for example, at a nubby fabric to comprehend that it *is* a nubby fabric. Often the window merchandise presentation of men's shops is handsome and neat, yet there is no bridge to the interior; the inside of the store remains blissfully unaware of what is on display in the windows. Sometimes the customer cannot easily find what is on display out front. If these techniques were used with other types of merchandise, they would be considered cliche, sub-standard and decidedly behind the times.

That men's wear departments and window displays are allowed to get into a "rut" and stay there is mostly the male customer's fault. He, being less frivolous, less conscious of change, less willing to accept change than the female, is satisfied to go along in an established pattern. If there is a surprising change, all right; but he never demands it. He likes things which are methodical and which speak of efficiency.

Every man has been educated from his very early years to the idea that he must make a place for himself in the world, must be a breadwinner, must be steeped in the essentials of building a successful business career. But to any man, 16 or 60, success means a lot more than job progress or high marks and campus intramurals. To him, success in dating the strawberry blonde with the blue eyes and being known as something the girls would whistle after if it were ladylike is just as important as an A grade or a compliment from the boss.

The wise display man themizes men's wear around the women in the customer's life. If cigarette companies can sell billions of less-nicotine-acid-tar tobacco products with a pretty girl, surely the display man can add more zest and appeal to men's apparel in much the same way.

For years now, women's apparel shops have been using mannequins or figures to show the merchandise. If mannequins are not too expensive for feminine apparel displays, they should not be forgotten in men's wear windows. In appealing to the woman, display artists install realistic backgrounds and use color techniques dramatically; in men's wear displays the background is more often wood paneling, polished geometric fixture settings or staid pedestals and statuary.

It is time for men's wear displays to be shaken out of the doldrums. Men go places—walk through the park, go to the ballgame and attend conventions. Men do things—make business appointments, dictate letters, dance, play with their kids, drive cars, read books, smoke pipes. Men are individuals—some like red-heads, others prefer blondes; some must see every murder movie which comes to town, others deem such activity a waste of time; some like to dress for dinner, others abhor it. Men sit on pieces of furniture at home and in their offices. Any one of these various situations could be used as a setting for a merchandise picture of men's wear. Why not present such merchandise in a dramatic setting once in a while, rather than on a straight ramrod form or precisely draped from a stand?

MASS MERCHANDISE

Another lost cause in display is "mass" merchandise. Some store owners feel compelled to stack, pile and place as much merchandise in their windows as possible. They either seem afraid the passer-by will not be shown every item that is inside the store; or they make a stockroom of their display areas by showing the entire case, all twenty boxes, stack upon stack of merchandise before the public. They believe that in units there is strength. There is no falser premise abroad today in the retailing field.

It is not necessary to display a gross of any item to get the message across to the customer. Focused attention on one item is much more powerful than on a dozen. Besides, the merchandise becomes more important if shown in smaller quantities. Tiffany has hundreds of diamonds, but they show their customers only one at a time.

Food stores, drug stores, hardware and novelty stores are in a retailing field that demands a certain amount of stacked merchandise or mass display. Such stores, especially self-service stores and supermarkets or discount houses, do not have carpeted floors and hidden stock areas like department stores or specialty salons.

The basis for success in mass merchandise stores is assortment, stock control and organized, inspiring display methods. The matter of stock control is not an accepted duty of the display man; it is more the concern of the buyer, the owner and the merchandising specialist. Unit stock control systems are the surest guide to shopper preferences and tastes; they catch volume right up with demand.

Stock control influences what the display men can and will do with the merchandise at hand. If an establishment has only so much stock space for surplus supplies and the merchandising man is offered a bargain car-load lot of merchandise which he purchases with no regard as to where he will keep the greater part of it while showing the customer a limited amount, the store is not using proper stock control methods. Because ten cases of Brand A soap arrived in the basement doesn't mean that all ten cases have to be plummeted into the area designated for soap on the selling floor. Likewise if Brand A soap sells much faster than Brand B, stock control methods advise against the reordering of equal amounts of Brand A and Brand B soap.

Important areas for display are the walls and the island tops of counters or superstructures. The walls are just above the reach of the customer but always in sight; the topped-off areas above the shelves or counters are beyond comfortable browsing height but are directly adjacent to a given item for sale. It is here that the display man should build his setting for the surrounding merchandise.

Sears, Roebuck & Co. has made extensive studies of customer reaction to self-service types of display. So if no ideas are forthcoming to your immediate need of mass display, by all means browse the champions of mass merchandising like Sear's or Kroger's.

No merchandise is too difficult to show appealingly and dramatically if a little thought, a great deal of effort and not too much money are invested in the problem. Consider a few display suggestions for mass merchandising:

Luggage is a type of merchandise akin to paint cans and automobile tires. The usual method for displaying luggage is to fill an area with as many different pieces as possible. However, luggage is a prime necessity for travel and travel is not dull; therefore, luggage should never become dull in display. Travel posters, timetables, cancelled tickets and stickers are free for the asking from most travel terminals. These add immeasurable atmosphere to luggage displays. Amid the stacks of luggage, one piece could be shown with appropriate items spilling out, thus showing the customer better, easier ways of packing, suggesting what he will need in the way of passport or legal papers when visiting foreign countries or displaying a wardrobe for a five-day cruise abroad. The illusory setting of a redcap's hands will lend appeal to this massive type of merchandise.

Everyone loves to receive mail, and far too few people write letters. A display which suggests that anyone may become a more charming letter writer with the proper kind of stationery, suggests that stationery is not just so many boxes and envelopes. Show stationery on a desk, near a waste basket or beside a quill pen which has just written "Dear Susan: The most wonderful thing has just happened . . ." to add animation to a mass display of merchandise.

The display possibilities for dog collars may seem trivial to most clerks. Usually these are hung on hooks in a very undramatic way. But when copy is added noting that this type of collar was worn by Sire A as Best of Breed in the recent dog show, or that this collar allows free movement and will not permit the leash to become entangled, or that this collar has a special plate for the dog's name as well as the owner's, then commonplace merchandise becomes of increasing interest to the passer-by.

The massed feeling in a homewares department may be relieved by associative merchandise or sketches in the background suggesting very real situations. A mannequin in furs shopping for a pie tin, a mannequin in formal evening dress whipping up an after-theatre snack in her kitchen, a mannikin in chef's cap and apron barbequing a steak for the neighborhood back yard crowd, a cook book open beside the mixing bowl, a hot pad near the newest aluminum skillet—all these things relieve the monotony of stack upon stack of homewares.

Screws become less a maze of bins full of massed items when associated with a need for their use. Screws are necessary for installing hinges. Screws certainly don't put themselves into surfaces, so a helpful screwdriver may be placed beside them for appeal. Every carpenter has to measure or mark exactly where

the screw is meant to go, so a measuring rule might be added to the display picture. The bins which segregate the types of screws might be varied from the usual square egg-crate effect and be made oblong and diamond-shaped—and even painted different colors to resemble a checker board. Behind the necessary bins there is usually ample space for a panel to permit dramatic display or suggestive selling features of hardware items.

Books, magazines, pamphlets and other reading materials of necessity become mass merchandise in their display areas. However, even such presentations may be relieved if a book is displayed here and there throughout a department related to the American reader and his leisure habits. Display technique turns down the corner of a page, opens the book on an end table and casually leaves a pair of glasses or a pipe nearby, or presents the books in a home-like atmosphere of shelves and book ends. The appearance of stack upon stack of books may be relieved by angling the stacks, stair-stepping the height of neighboring piles, or using odd numbers wherever possible.

Zippers are a wonderful invention, but how many notions departments ever show them except as a mass item? It is all wrong to use a skirt placket zipper in a dress or a heavy weight zipper with voile or nylon materials, so the customer might be reminded of this in an attractive display. He should be shown, too, that zipper tapes are dyed to match the myriad colors of each season's fabrics. A sewing room scene with tape measure, dress form and other dressmaker accessories will foster the sale of more zippers.

Stacks of towels become less staid and more romantic when several of them are tied up brightly with wide pieces of ribbon. Bedding is more personal when an item is shown monogrammed. Down comforts, draped over a cedar chest or in front of a wintry window scene, suddenly become a part of the customer's daily needs instead of simply silk and satin on a shelf.

Paint is so very unromantic, yet display men are able to glamorize even such mass merchandise. Ladders displaying paint cans on their rungs will sell two house improvement needs in one display. A paper plate painted

27 WINDOW SIGNS

with a clock face and placed atop a pyramid stack of cans with a bit of copy nearby stating "Now is the time to think of remodeling" will attract the passer-by more often than a stack of lonely paint cans. When a display suggests sandpaper surgery for peeling walls or chipped paint, it also arouses a trend of thought in the mind of the customer which will bring him back to that source for sandpaper when he has a need for it.

The very simplest use for merchandise is often the easiest way to promote its sale. Many times the solution to a display problem is so simple that it is laughable. Take for example the automatic pencil company which had spent hundreds of dollars and much time trying to prepare a television commercial in which the pencil was suspended at a writing angle on stationery. Wires were used, frameworks were built and many intricate methods of display were tried. This baffling problem was solved simply by removing the lead from the barrel of the pencil and slipping it over the shaft of a straight pin which had been tapped into a soft surface at the desired angle.

Merchandising is fascinating. It becomes more fascinating every time a problem in display is met and solved.

COPY

Solving copy problems in display brings up another lost cause. Copy may be defined as any type of sign, and the words thereon, that is used with a display to explain the merchandise shown or to relate it to something that may prompt the customer to buy. (See *Figure 27*.) A display without good copy is like a newspaper made up of photographs alone without a line of information about any of them. Window displays are not usually so lacking in good copy as are the interiors of stores and their various departments.

Stores may have too many signs with price tags and at the same time be lacking in pertinent selling lines of copy in relation to the merchandise. Tables or counters topped with signs stating: "Slacks $7.98," "Shoes $4.79," "Blouses $2.98," "Pans 98c" lack customer appeal, and such signs merely add to the massed conglomeration of fixtures and merchandise.

Signs are the silent salesmen in every department. They take the place of the clerk out on his lunch hour. They can do a good promotional job because they are the follow-through on advertising and TV continuity. Copy lends character and personality to the display of merchandise.

Copy is to a merchandising picture what frosting is to a cake or mushroom dressing to a steak. It is the finishing touch, the artist's signature to an interesting study in merchandise. This signature of words may be placed on a sign equal in size to that of a calling card or on paper and mat board as large as a billboard. These signs may cover a wall area or be simply a price ticket placed on the merchandise. The pertinent fact is that too many department managers, too many store owners, become nonchalant about their copy situation and overlook its importance.

Knox, New York

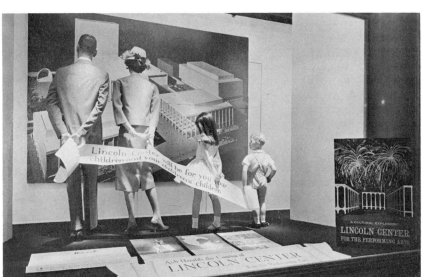

R. H. Macy & Co., New York

Abraham & Straus, New York

The requirements for effective signs are that they be informative, accurate, appropriate, follow a set pattern and avoid verbosities.

Information given on a sign must be interesting as well as accurate. Copy invites the passer-by to hesitate and investigate merchandise placed with the sign. There is no excuse for incorrect spelling. Most copy originates in the departments from which the merchandise comes. This is a natural sequence since the buyer chooses the merchandise as a result of a manufacturer's salesmanship and these salesmanship techniques may be emphasized to the customer. Such procedure assures the accuracy of information regarding sizes, colors, irregulars, price, etc. If buyers and department managers do not take an interest in writing better copy, the display man must gently assist them toward more colorful wording.

Nor is the display man content to place a sign in his windows which simply says "Summer Story" or "Pink Is Such a Subtle Color." Eye-catching phrases should be supplemented with additional copy to relate them to the merchandise at hand. The choice of appropriate signs to meet a given situation is a definite requirement of a good signing policy in any store. Assuredly, a huge sign should not be placed in a shadow box display of fountain pens, nor should a small price tag be the only copy notation in a large window.

House cards placed on counters and tables in various departments of a store usually fall into the standard sizes of one-eighth, one-fourth, full sheets, etc. Either the vertical or the horizontal format may be employed, but the heavy content of the copy on any sign should be in the lower right quarter of the card. The accepted pattern for most house signs is that each card shall contain a pre-heading, a main heading or lead line, two or three pertinent facts and the price. Following are several examples:

Poor Copy Writing

LAMPS

$24.98 Pr.

NEW OVERALLS

$4.98

BRIGHT TABLECLOTHS

$3.79

Better Copy Writing

For Better Lighting
BOUDOIR LAMPS

17-inch base
etched design
four colors

$24.98 Pair

For Cold Weather
CORDUROY OVERALLS

adjustable straps
pin-wale design
sizes 2 to 6

$4.98

Tri-Color Scheme
BREAKFAST CLOTHS

pure linen crash
fast colors
51" × 51"

$3.79

However, there is no definite pattern for window signs to follow. Each store sets its own policy. Some adhere to formal mat board cards, others prefer script-written floppies. A floppy is a flimsy type of background for copy which, when placed other than on the wall or floor, tends to flop down just as it is placed. Parchment, pebble-finish bond paper or even stationery sheets may become floppy-type signs. Thus, signs for the various display areas of a store might include floppys, streamers, cards, hat tags, etc., depending on the amount of copy needed for the merchandise shown. (See *Figure 27*).

Copy should not be too curt if it is to be effective, nor should it be verbose. Signs full of trivialities hinder rather than help in selling merchandise. Likewise, signs which merely state the price of an article are only an enlarged price tag and in no way help to create a mood for the customer; they do not suggest why the customer should buy a certain article and what it will do for him—in his home, in his office, while traveling.

Fashion magazines and trade journals are sources for pieces of copy. Trade journals present information to the retailer months before it is to be released to the customer and therefore keep the copy writer abreast of the times. Fashion magazines are wells of new ideas, coming trends and smart copy. Copy found in a jewelry advertisement could be transposed so as to accommodate a sprightly description of toys, apparel or homewares. The display man discovers pert phrases in many places if he will but stop and consider. Several pages in the appendix of this book offer suggestions for better copy writing. They are not complete window or departmental signs, but they will channel the thinking processes toward more dramatic copy writing.

The bigger department stores use parchment, expensive mat board and no-seam paper for their signing jobs. The small store owner might use pastel-colored stationery attached to an attractive shirt box lid, with copy written in crayon, chalk or the new magic-marker type felt-tipped pen, just as effectively. All stores should analyze their present copy and sign situation to be sure that it is not just another lost cause in modern display techniques.

These lost causes in display need more champions to study them. Any small store owner can improve the status of these lost causes if he will but try earnestly.

10 New Horizons Beckon

There is no greater challenge to young people in retailing today than display. The success of a venture depends upon how well those involved in its various aspects do their job. The horizons beckoning in display work are far-reaching and endless in possibilities.

TRAINING FOR DISPLAY

In the early days of display, a window trimmer's job was purely accidental. A display man wasn't trained—he was trapped. An unsuspecting clerk was told to trim the windows, or anyone free on Tuesday morning changed the merchandise in the front display areas. The display man today is a professional. His work is the most important phase of merchandising within the walls of a retailing establishment. Yet his work is so casual, so well mastered in relation to the store and its merchandise, that few customers are ever aware of his artistic efforts—until they are taken away.

Because display techniques must be applied to store premises with great care and purpose in order to be effective, the display man often finds himself a "Jack-of-all-trades." Today, the display worker is part merchant in that he knows what his store has to sell and where to find it; he is part psychologist for he analyzes customer habits and evaluates their reactions to a given situation; he is part artist in that he applies the theory of design and color; he is part engineer and craftsman for he must install lighting effects and fashion old materials into better display settings; and finally, he is part executive for he helps establish store policy and coordinates promotional themes throughout the store.

Such increasing demands on the display profession have established it as one of the most versatile and all-encompassing branches of merchandising. Training and education in as many related fields as possible is important to the individual considering display as a profession.

Various cities across the nation offer display courses through their distributive education plans, retail training institutes or special night classes. Such courses are usually short and lack the laboratory work so necessary for a complete understanding of display, but they are a good beginning.

Many colleges list display courses in their regular yearly curricula. New York University, Stephens College, Traphagen School of Fashion and the University of Southern California are but four of some fifty colleges throughout America which offer detailed study in display.

Of all the institutions which specialize in display education, the National Display Institute of Philadelphia, Pennsylvania, is one of the most thorough and outstanding. The Institute was begun on an experimental basis in 1948, and present facilities contain huge workshops in window technique, silk screening, papier mache, wood-working, etc. As a part of their training, students at the Institute work in local department stores and meet the very real problems of display. The Institute believes in education and book knowledge, but it also contends that knowledge without application is of little use to anyone.

There are several correspondence schools which give courses in display techniques. One of the oldest is the Koester School in Chicago, Illinois; another is the Will H. Bates school at Ellsworth, Illinois. Both offer detailed printed courses with sketches and application suggestions.

WORK IN THE FIELD

Practical application is of prime importance to the education of any individual in display techniques. In his realm of make-believe and merchandise pictures, the display man strives for the odd, the diversified, the variant. Each situation, each season, each year brings new problems to be considered and understood. Display is one of the few artisan trades in modern business which encourages apprentice training. In fact, many of the best display men in America began as a helper's helper in some display department.

Display is no place for primadonnas. It is a creative, dignified profession, but its workers must be willing to face the less glamorous tasks—carrying fixtures, dressing mannequins and hunting props—as well as the creative labors of design, color and art. As in all professions, well trained and adept persons are sought and too seldom found.

A good display man must be a carpenter, electrician, stagehand and a painter all rolled into one, or at least he must know how to direct these various jobs. In a field where much of the work includes hammering, sawing, moving fixtures and climbing ladders. it is only natural that the personnel has been predominantly male. Men far outnumber women in display departments. It is interesting to note, however, that more and more women are entering this profession, a fact which is most gratifying since there are many tasks in display where a woman's touch is needed: window accessorist, designer, artist and fashion coordinator, for example.

FASHION SHOWS

Almost every display department, at one time or another, has been called upon to stage a fashion show. Fashions are very important to the woman shopper. Consequently, the tastefully set presentation of what is style for a given season, for the campus crowd, for the Easter Parade, for the bride or for the nursery set, is becoming a more frequent phase in the over-all picture of visual merchandising.

In the old days, a fashion show consisted simply of models walking on a stage or moving about among the customers in a salon to the tune of "Lovely To Look At." The modern fashion show has a script, a runway, perhaps a complete background setting, lighting effects, music, pretty models showing pretty clothes and sometimes tea and crumpets afterward. Fashion shows are a prestige event for any store. They relate merchandise and show the ensemble look rather than segregated items. They are an important factor for increased sales and are definitely worth all the work which is done behind the scenes to make them possible. To be outstanding, to become important to the community, fashion shows must be interesting, relaxing, glamorous and, above all, well planned and executed.

The theme is one of the most important elements of any fashion show. Once the title of the show is decided upon, whether it be Young Fashions, The Nursery Set, Easter Parading, The Coke Crowd, Bon Voyage or some other, the theme must be perpetrated throughout the show. Continuity is best developed by dividing the merchandise to be modeled into various groups. Casual wear for college may be shown, then classroom wear, then fraternity life and social dressing needs may be demonstrated, and then the classic styles for football; every part integrated into a pleasant merchandise picture afoot.

The setting of a style show is closely tied to the theme. The setting should never overshadow the merchandise. It should be simple and dramatic. If it is simple, the business of dismantling afterwards is less of a problem. If it is dramatic, the task of maintaining interest and carrying that interest right back to the departments from which the merchandise came is more easily accomplished. A central prop of gigantic proportions is the easiest set to prepare for a fashion show. The magazine stand in a railway station, the ornate gateway to some formal garden, the soda bar at the corner drug store, or satin pouffs with actual salon effects are but a few of the easier settings to use.

If the fashion show is presented in a department, a carpeted runway with a small atmosphere piece at one end and a spot light or two added for dramatic effect will suffice. Folding chairs are set up and the show goes on.

The commentary which accompanies the show should be coordinated with both theme and set. Long scripts and lengthy introductions are not accepted protocol at fashion shows. Quick notes about outstanding points of the ensemble are usually jotted down on cards and referred to by the commentator. A script should never be read in its entirety. Ad-libbing to keep pace with a turn of the model or a placing of her hand in a pocket will emphasize a point much more clearly than many flowery words. It is best for the commentator to present models in a sequence which will allow each one ample time for changing into the next outfit. Tight time schedules can be nerve-racking to backstage personnel.

Music adds glamour to fashion shows, but it should never supersede the commentator. Music is present for effect and to relax the models in their promenading. It is most appropriate when presented in undertone. A piano or an organ have much more style than an inadequate orchestra. It is wise to avoid somber and overly gay tunes. Semi-classic and hit tunes of the day are most appropriate.

Proper announcement and advertising of the show is one phase of fashion show coordination which many merchandising men overlook, but this work must be done if the presentation is to be a success. Clerks in the various departments participating in the style show should make it a point to invite their customers personally to the coming show; newspaper announcements should be run a week before the show and again on the day of the event. Radio, TV and window announcements of the fashion show should come a day or two before the show itself.

Printed programs are optional at style shows. Many times they help the audience keep in step with the progress of the show. Also, they are a handy reference for the customer when she visits the apparel shops afterwards to purchase merchandise presented. Mailing lists should not be overlooked as a possibility for advertising a fashion show.

The display man is the one who naturally inherits a large responsibility for the presentation of fashion shows. It is a part of his job and should not be overlooked any more than windows, interiors, or television commercials.

TELEVISION

The most recent star on the horizon beckoning to display workers is television. The many aspects of television production definitely need and invite display artists to join the ranks of video. Such phases of TV production as commercials, background flats, actual sets, lighting and color quality are factors which the display man understands and works with every time he installs a merchandise picture in any department of his store.

It goes without saying that television, being a one-time proposition, needs people with ideas for creating background illusion quickly and inexpensively, without actually constructing these backgrounds in detail. TV seeks personnel who have dozens of ideas for the use of a single prop and who are capable of refinishing it or adding to it by simple construction, people with the ingenuity for fashioning effective substitutes for more expensive, weighty props. Who can meet these qualifications better than the display man?

In the production of commercials for TV, all the basic theories of display are applied to arrangement, dramatic effect and demonstration. The viewing audience is not satisfied to be told simply: "Here is a fine doughnut cutter;" they want to be shown. Demonstration is proving to be the secret of successful, sales-pulling commercials. Wordy promises in TV commercials only perpetuate low sales figures; demonstrations of the product and proof of its value doubles and triples sales figures. In TV commercials using table-top, turntable, flip, crawl or proscenium titles,* the display man is past master. These are only variations of the technique he applies in window floppies or departmental signing. The biggest problem in TV commercial production is reducing the amount of copy used without sapping the strength of the message.

Television programs are composed mostly of series of separate close-up shots, so any background used must blend or fade into the entire picture. Sets are colored in soft, greyed tones so they do not jump out at the camera. Just as in display, the merchandise is dominant and the background remains an illusion. The elements of TV production, like travelers, flats, cycloramas and painted sets,† are second nature to the display man who spends the majority of his time placing merchandise in dramatic settings. He can very easily adjust his art to accommodate live actors or merchandise to be placed before the camera.

Set designing and construction is most important to any TV show. On close inspection, the props used on musical or comedy shows prove to be mostly suggested effects—a post here, a step

---

* . . . *flip titles* are printed, lettered cards which fall before the TV camera, one after another, to form a continuous message.

. . . *crawl titles* are rolled on a drum in continuous script fashion around the camera.

. . . *proscenium titles* feature a miniature stage showing cards, one at a time, until the last card falls, revealing the opening scene of the program.

---

† . . . traveler: a movable background on pulleys.

. . . flats: background panels constructed of wood and cloth.

. . . cyclorama: a canvas backdrop hanging in folds to infer background effects.

there, foliage drooping. The initial connotation is made and the mind of the viewer immediately fills in the details with related thought patterns. Too much or too little decoration would detract from these settings.

Many of the third vice presidents in the store management today with the title of promotion director or publicity coordinator began their coordinating and promoting in display departments. The backgrounds of many outstanding cartoonists, mannequin designers and free-lance store planners can be traced to a display department beginning.

It follows from all this that display horizons are endless. As trends change, so display changes. The future importance of display is limited only by the vision and enthusiasm of the young men and women who choose to take up the profession. The person who can be an artist and yet is not too "artistic" should be in display. The person who has different ideas—not too "different"—and a desire to please people should certainly investigate the possibilities of display. The person who has an earnest will to work and a flair for creative living is needed in display. The art of doing is the art of living and that is the art of display.

11 Examples of Good Display Techniques

We are aware of the important scientific studies which seek a sound barrier breakthrough, a radiation breakthrough, a space breakthrough. We of merchandising should become adept at the art of display breakthrough.

Display breakthrough for merchandising is twofold. First there is the need for an idea. Just where do ideas come from in display; how are novel display treatments begun? Second, there is the need for a change in technique or execution.

Ideas are the molecular basis for explosions which result in more sales and more goods sold. And sometimes the solution or idea for a display is so simple that it may be easily overlooked.

May I mention a problem of my own. We were to have a beige fashion promotion one Spring. An entire battery of 12 windows were to be used for blouses, shoes, dresses, sportswear and related items, all in the tone of beige or cream. I was nearly desperate for an idea. How trite to say Basic Beige or some such advertising idea. One Sunday I happened into a drug store with some friends. We were ordering around and I asked for vanilla ice cream. Another spoke up "Who wants vanilla? Chocolate for me." And there an idea was born. We used a soda fountain set with children and the grown up merchandise. The town is still talking about it, and the copy card, "Who Wants Vanilla?"

The important thing is not always to give in to the doldrum of the usual. Granted, not every display you make will be a riproaring success. But the will not always to do it the same way is half the battle won.

We were talking of breakthroughs. Why not have one right there in one of your windows, or on a mirror in your shop some day?

Break a tree limb with foliage on it through your display area. Of course, you don't actually break the pane; you simply put part of the tree or limb inside the glass and part of it outside on the street or in the foyer or on the mirror. A bit of felt on the pane-touching surfaces and some hidden wires and you're in business. Place a bird on the limb and play a twittering bird record now and then. (Cornell University has some delightful ones.)

Be sure to check town ordinances and ask clearance through the safety director of your area. They are usually most helpful. And police departments keep an eye on urchins with malicious intent. Then, too, you always place the breakthrough technique well above the six foot level.

The ability to associate ideas with merchandise in proper sequence is hard work as is everything successful. But the selling power of display depends on how attractively the stage is set for the merchandise.

Any season of the year is packed with ideas. Summer boating and fun. Your diamond rings taped to live turtle backs in an aquarium. The country fair and your blue ribbon winners in any class. Kites in the Spring flying high with tails made of watch bands. A Christmas tree alive with fruit or note papers. People are influenced by the season, the weather; and people are customers.

Associate the known with the unknown. A customer may have never tried the non-skid binding you sell, but she has slipped on the bathroom rug, so put the two together. Consider the thought changes brought about in the mind of the customer to whom you are trying to promote grey—grey anything—when you prefix the grey display card with slate, pewter, charcoal, dawn, etc.

Often the merchandise itself will suggest an idea. The special inside treatment of ceramics, the brand name, Victorian chintz, French lace, Japanese prints—all simply but immediately set up a mental picture which you can use as the stage or display presentation for that merchandise.

Following are some fine photographic examples of outstanding displays. They are but a pebble in the river of display ideas that come off the drawing boards weekly.

I thought you might like to browse through them for breakthroughs in better and more exciting techniques.

Women's Apparel Displays

Bloomingdale's, New York

Hochschild Kohn & Co., Baltimore

Saks Fifth Avenue, New York

86

L. Brandeis & Sons, Omaha   Neiman-Marcus, Houston

Maison Blanche, New Orleans   The Vogue, Flint

Bonwit Teller, Philadelphia

Miller's, Knoxville

Gimbel Brothers, Philadelphia

Forbes & Wallace, Springfield

89

Garrard & Co., London

Woodward & Lothrop, Washington

Lit Brothers, Philadelphia

Men's Apparel Displays

Meyers & McCarthy, Fort Wayne

92

Sterling Lindner Co., Cleveland

Woodward & Lothrop, Washington

Christy & Co., London

Children's Apparel Displays

Stern's, New York

Saks Fifth Avenue, New York

95

Stern's, New York

Orbach's, New York

Bloomingdale's, New York

97

Home Furnishings
and Appliance Displays

Lord & Taylor, New York

Bloomingdale's, New York

Stern's, New York

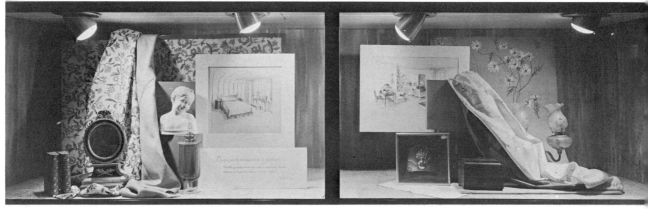

Public Service E & G Co., Newark

Washington Gas Light Co., Washington

Ohio Edison Co., Springfield

Commonwealth Edison Co., Chicago

E. J. Korvette, Brooklyn

Stern's, New York

Domestics, Linens, China
and Glassware Displays

Bloomingdale's, New York

Lord & Taylor, New York

Lord & Taylor, New York

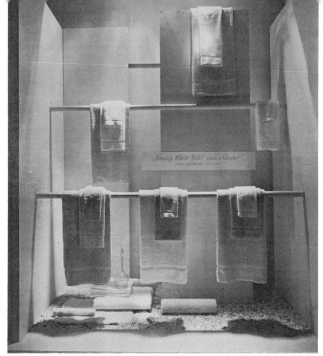

Bloomingdale's, New York

Stern's, New York

The Crescent, Spokane

107

108

INDEPENDENCEWHITEIRONSTONEDINNERWAREBYCASTLETON5-PIECEPLACESETTINGS.25CHINASECONDFLOOR
Gump's

109

Steuben Glass, New York

W. & J. Sloane, New York

R. H. Macy & Co., New York

Special Events and Seasonal Displays

Ohrbach's, La Mirada

Maison Blanche, New Orleans

Lord & Taylor, New York

R. H. Macy & Co., New York

Pogue's, Cincinnati

Marshall Field & Co., Wauwatosa   B. Altman, New York

Marshall Field & Co., Wauwatosa   B. Altman, New York

Woodward & Lothrop, Washington   The Crescent, Spokane

113

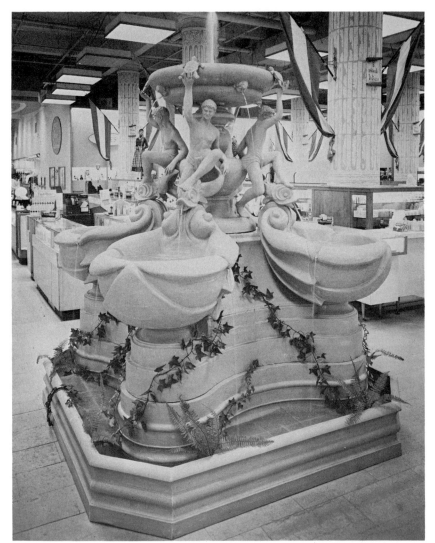

Maison Blanche, New Orleans

B. Gertz, Jamaica

Special Displays

Harris Trust and Savings Bank, Chicago

The Knox, Knoxville

Displaycraft, Long Island City

Radio Corporation of America, New York

The Myer Emporium, Melbourne

Morgan Piano Co., Miami

EVERYTHING IS GO

An Afterthought

Collected in the following pages are supplementary facts and bits of information which will broaden the reader's comprehension of the display field. For the student, they are awesome yet very necessary and should be considered with the purpose of further enlightenment. For the person already in display, they are to be plucked and feathered as specific needs or problems arise on the daily production scene.

Suggested Copy

"In a large sense one would say there is no pure originality. All minds quote. Old and new make the warp and woof of every moment. We quote not only books and proverbs, but arts, sciences, religion, customs and laws; nay, we quote temples and houses, tables and chairs, by imitation."
. . . Ralph Waldo Emerson

Consider the blind man in front of the Waldorf Astoria Hotel in New York City asking favor with the sign:

I am Blind

Then consider the same situation with a sign:

It is Spring
and
I am Blind

Assuredly it is easy to understand that his intake from the second sign will almost double that from the first.

The following bits of suggestive copy are not complete. They are simple "lead" lines to spark further thought in relation to a specific need for words with merchandise on display.

ACCESSORIES
Center of Attraction (Belts)
Something to Draw Straws Over (Straw Hats)
Made for Each Other
Spring Headlines
Accented with Color
For the Pretty Waist
Handbags with Vocations

Just the Thing for Flying Tresses
Fashion Touches
Glamour at Your Fingertips (Gloves)
Scarfs Are So Versatile
A Young Hand Fancies . . . (Gloves)
Stocking Beauty
Pick Accessories that Harmonize
Gay Figured Neckwear
Billowy White and Sheer (Blouses)
Pocket Highlights (Hankies)
Exquisite Handmade Patterns
Seamless Sheerness (Hosiery)
Leg Art in Pastel Shades
Petite Evening Accents
Color in Your Seams (Hosiery)

BOOKS and STATIONARY
Write on Fine Paper
Nothing Takes the Place of a Letter
When You're Away
Write a Line a Day
The Pleasing Gift
A Paper Trousseau for the Bride
Someone Has a Birthday Today
Reading Can Be Fun
Pleasant Thoughts for Leisure Hours
Personalized Stationery (Monogramming)
Colored Ink to Accentuate
Fun for All the Family
Treasured Memories (Scrapbooks)
In the Spotlight (Photo Albums)
On the Book Beat
A Grab Bag of Fact and Fiction

Helpful Guides to Modern Art
A New Addition to a Popular Series

THE BRIDE
Young Married's
Third Finger, Left Hand
Suggestions for the Groom
It's Brides' Week at . . .
Down the Center Aisle
Here Comes the Bride
Cherished Memories
For the Newlyweds
Honeymoon Secrets
Lovely to Look at
Cupid's Calling
As Traditional as the Wedding Ring
For Wedding Belles
She'll Love, Honor and Cherish . . .
Every Bride Is a Hostess-To-Be
Remember the Bride with a Shower of . . .
To Lighten the Bride's Homework
The Modern Bride Chooses "Something New"
Durable Dreams
Along Your Bridal Path
Trans-Seasoned Traveler

CAMPUS LIFE and FALL PROMOTIONS
We Polish the Pupil
Campus Bound
The Three R's
* —Rugged*
* —Ready*
* —Reliable*
In a Class by Itself
Booked for Fall
Stadium Stunners
Make Class History
Campus Stars
For Labs and Lassies
Jack Frost Specials
A Harvest of . . .
Get Ready for Fall
For the Coke Crowd
Active and Attractive
Take Your Major in . . . (Wool, Tweeds)
Classroom Winners
For College & Career
Coordinated Campus Wardrobe
From Science to Sodas

CHILDREN'S APPAREL
Togs for Reluctant Little Dragons
We Major in Minors
The Kiddies Love . . .
Your Child Needs . . .

Cut Kiddie Clothes Costs
Your Baby Deserves the Best
What's Your I.Q. on Infants?
Chubbie Charm
Prissy Little Missy
For Monday Morning Rascals
Appearance for Eye Appeal
Priced for Buy Appeal
For the Junior Members of the Wedding
The Smock Look

CHRISTMAS
For the Head of Your Christmas List
And the Foot of Your Christmas Tree
It's Gifts Like These that Turn a Woman's Head
Yuletide Hints
Bundle Up Your Love for Christmas
Christmas Bliss for a Teen-Age Miss
Merry Christmas in a Woman's Language
Gifts to Make You Her Favorite Santa
Booty for Your Beauty
Like Wrapping Her in Cotton Puffs
Santa Approved
Finer Toys for Good Little Girls and Boys
It's Fun to Make Christmas Gifts
Christmas All Through the House
Happy Holiday
For Giving and Getting
Under the Tree
So Many Lovely Ways of Saying Merry Christmas
Wrap Up Your Christmas Male
Straight From Santa Claus
Merry Christmas, Darling!
Tells a Gala Christmas Story

COLOR
Skipper Blue
Symphony in . . .
A Windfall of Wonderful Colors
Urban Black
A Carnival of Colors
Spotlight on . . .
Blue—Darkly, Deeply, Beautifully Blue
American Beauties in January
Spiked with Cinnamon
Cardinal Red
All the Colors in the Rainbow
Rich, Soft Colors
A Strong Navy
In the Pink
Pastel Accents
A Tropical Paradise of Color
Demitasse Brown
24 Karat Gold
Dynamite Red Plays Havoc with Jet Black

New Neutrals in Almond Tones
Beautiful Beige
Pale Sand

COSMETICS
For Hands and Body
Trust . . . (Brand Name)
Liquid Splendor
Look Younger Again
Surface Camouflage
Instantly You Are so Much Lovelier
Want to Look Beautiful?
In Moonlight—In Sunlight
New Life for Your Complexion
Restyle Your Face
Take a Second Look
All That's New and Important in Make-Up
Stop, Look and Reconsider
For Sea, Sun and Shenanigans
Beauty Is Your Business
Everyday—Let Fragrance Be Yours
Your Crowning Glory
Choose a Powder Base with Care
For Professional Home Care
Memo To Yourself
On Friendly Terms with Your Skin

ELECTRICAL APPLIANCES and HOMEWARES
Meals to Crow About
For Meals that Make a Husband Boast
Have a Carefree Kitchen
For Purses of All Sizes
Color Cues for Smart Kitchens
Packed with Value
Cooking Can Be Fun
The Heart of Any Kitchen
Makes Kitchen Duty a Pleasure
Freeze It—Save It
Automatic . . . Economical
Beautify Your Kitchen
Mother's Little Helpers
The World at Your Finger Tips
Best House Paint to Use
Makes a Hit with Homemakers
Worth Its Weight in Gold
Compact, Thrifty and Dependable
Practical Gifts for the Bride
Making Housework Fun

FABRICS
Color Is Your Best Buy
California by the Yard
It's Pouring Plaids
Get Into Print

Window Glamour
Pick a Pattern
Cloud Soft
Fresh-Cut Flowers
Denim Does It
Crisp Freshness of Texture
Easy to Sew . . . Easy to Launder
A Dash of Glamour in Your Room's Costume
Cheer Up Your House with Color
It's Amazing What You Can Do with Figures
Fabrics for Color—Fabrics for Drama
Pin-Stripe Neatness
Big Splashes of Color for Your Walls
Sewing Can Be Fun
Home Sewing Cuts Budget Costs for Clothes
Create the Illusion of Space
Crisp as Lettuce Cottons
Wearable Woolens
Glamour in Gingham

FURNITURE
For More Gracious Living
Colors to Compliment Any Dining Room
A Joy to Have Around the House
A Roomful of Color
Cheer Up Your House
Collector's Items
More Graceful Contour
Wonderful Tricks with Color
The Well-Spent Dollar
For Lifetime Pleasure
Ready for Unexpected Company
Enjoy the Enduring Loveliness of FURNITURE
Masterpieces that Anyone Can Enjoy
Bedroom Beauty Begins
For Comfortable Living
Glorify Your Home
Decorative Treasures for Every Home
Tops in Quality
The Ace of Home Economy
Budget Prices
Smart Design
When Luxury Is a Bargain

JEWELRY
Master Craftsmen
Exquisite Design
None so Precious as . . .
To Fit Your Neck Perfectly
The Golden Manner
Brilliant Styling
Sparkling Allure
Gifts Galore
Fetching Femininity
For Party Excitement
Ear-resistable Splendor

Delicate Sculpture
Scintillating Reflections of Your Charm
Lovely Creations
Precious Metals and Rare Gems
Breath-Taking Beauty
Symbols of Beauty
Chalk White
Coined for Your Wrist
Pinned Forever
A Hint of Romance
The Eastern Influence

LINENS
Tricks with Your Table
A Touch of Magic for Your Table
Fairy Godmother to Your Dreams
Mealtime Magic
For Family Dining
Mealtime Adventures
A Cozy Twosome
Come On, Let's Eat!
For a Busy Hostess
Conversation Pieces
Linens for Her Hope Chest
The . . . Label Protects Your Table
If You Are a Shade Romantic
Give the New Homemaker . . .

LINGERIE
A Delightful Wisp of Sheer . . .
Winning-Look Colors
Styling in Line and in Color
New, Longer-Wearing Features
A Flair for Fashion
A Genius for Giving Comfort
To Wear Under Everything
Underlined
Under Cover
Beautiful Belittlers
For Sleeping Beauties
Shapelier Curves
A Wisp of Sheerness
Molds the Figure
Proportionately Yours
Nylon Gives You Something Extra
Sheer Delight
Start of a Lovelier Figure
For a Private Life
Notice Your Slimmer Waistline
Breathtakingly Lovely
Blessed with Fragile Lace
Want To Be a Bedtime Cinderella?

MEN'S WEAR
Is POP the Question?
You'll Find the Answer Here

For the Man of the House
Make Mine Ties, Please
Cater to Pater
For Active Outdoor Men
For Work or Play
Clothes Make the Man
Accessories Make the Clothes
Style for Street and Office
Look Your Best in Any Weather
Your Guide to Good Grooming
Smartly Informal
Daring Styling
Details Make the Difference
Symbolic of Painstaking Craftsmanship
Favorite Leisure-Wear

MISCELLANEOUS
The Change of Pace
. . . Breaks Into Print
An Array of . . .
. . . Takes Over
Companions to . . .
There's No Better Time
Inside Story of . . .
Terrific
Something New
Smart Economy
Stamp of Approval
. . . on Parade
Toast of the Town
Enchantment
Look, We've Caught Tomorrow
Portrait of You for . . .
Best in the Show
Everyone's Talking About . . .
Invitation to Laughter
A Word to the Wise
It's a Wonderful Buy
Style as Modern as Surrealism
How to Leave Home and Like It (Luggage)

SHOES
Shoes Give a Costume Personality
Alluring Footwear
Smart Shoemaking Art
Fashions at Your Feet
Beautifully Paired
Strap Sorcery
On You—On Your Friends
A Little Magic with Leather
Any Way You Look at Them
Flatter Your Feet
For Dramatic Emphasis
For Those Dancing Feet
They Barely Ring the Toes
Designs for Focal Beauty

With Seeming Slimness
Fashion and Fit from Heel to Toe
The High and Low Notes of Footwear
Delicately Poised on a Platform
Color Sequence for Spring
The Basic Go-Everywhere Shoe
In Every Woman's Wardrobe
Something New Under Foot
Shoes That Stir Excitement
Wherever You Go

SILVERWARE
Teatime Treasures
Shining Symbol of Hospitality
Loveliness for Your Table
Lasting Beauty
Lifetime Pleasure
Wonderful Patterns
Crisp Beauty of Detail
Versatile Charm
Enjoy Day After Day
To Cherish Throughout the Years
Now Is the Time to Start Collecting
Give Her Silver She'll Love thc Rest of Her Life
Silver Gives Grace to the Dinner Table
Two's Company
When the Table's Set with Silver
Its Beauty Increases with Wear
Craftsmanship Is Important
Eloquent Simplicity
Luster For Your Table

SPRING and EASTER
Gay as the Queen of May
Up in the Sky So High
Swing Into Another Season
Mr. Bunny's Fashion for Young Things
Soft as Spring Air
Easter Wrappings
Eggs-actly What She Wanted
Reflections on Spring (Written on a Mirror)
Our Prophecy for Spring
A Pre-Spring Look
First Chirp of Spring
Soft as a Breath of Spring
Spring Bursts Forth
High Fashion for Spring
On Wings of Spring
First Place in the Easter Parade
Mr. Bunny Comes to Town
Spring Is Just Around the Corner

SUB-DEB
Two Is Company
To Live In—To Love In

It's a Date
Beau-Getters
Teen-Age Dandy
Sweet as Candy
The Young Slant on Clothes
For a Gala Gathering
Party Stealers
Put Your Prettiest Foot Forward
More Fun Than a Barrel of Monkeys
After-Five Drama
High, Wide and Then Some
A Dream of a Buy
Younger Than Springtime
Party-Going Casuals
Sophisticated Charm
Tea-Time, Fun-Time Clothes
Well-Groomed, But Ever So Casual

SUMMER and VACATION
To Bloom in the Sun
Sun White
For Sun, Fun and Frolic
Have Your Back to the Sun
For When the City Simmers
Icy Cool
Calm, Cool and Collected
Water Babies
Spic 'n' Span
Two Week Vacation with Play
Heavenly Cool
Sun-sational
To Sea and Be Seen
For Summer Knights
Around the Sun Dial
A Mid-Summer Hit
All Sails Set for a Cool Summer
Fashions That Go South
Mid-Summer Day's Dream
Vacation Playmates
Designed with a Southern Accent
Out-dorables
Let's See Your Sea Legs
Light as Chinese Parchment
Cool As Shade
Inside Story for Outdoor Living

WOMEN'S WEAR
Cotton for the Country,
But with Plans for Commuting
Sapling Slim and Sheer
For Raining Glory
Suits to Steal a March on . . .
May We Help You with Your Coat, Madame?
For Line, For Fabric
The Season's Newest Silhouette

Ready to Wear with Pleasure
Fashioned In Paris
Easy to Look at
Slim as a Soda Straw
Day In and Day Out
A . . . that's Wonderful to Wear
Focus on Front Fullness
Barebacks
Present Mood—Future Tense
Cool as a Frosted Cucumber
A Wonderful Line-up of . . .
Magnificent Fabrics
Suit Perfection
New Arrivals
Welcome and Wearable
That Band Box Look
Exciting To See . . . To Wear
The Little Weather-or-Not Coat
Blouses—So <u>*Suitable*</u>

**SOME SPECIAL EVENTS AROUND WHICH
PROMOTIONS MAY BE USED**
New Year's Day
Lincoln's Birthday
Valentine's Day
Washington's Birthday
Mardi Gras
Ash Wednesday
St. Patrick's Day
Palm Sunday
Easter
Mother's Day
Memorial Day
Graduation
Flag Day
Father's Day
Independence Day
Friendship Day
Labor Day
Columbus Day
Jewish New Year
Sweetest Day
Hallowe'en
Thanksgiving
Chanukah
Christmas
Scout Week
Baby Week
Book Week
Fire Prevention Week
Fair Week
Pre-Inventory Sale
Anniversary Sale
Homecoming
Confirmation

ANNIVERSARIES

1st	Paper
2nd	Cotton
3rd	Leather
4th	Books, Fruit, Flowers
5th	Wood
6th	Iron, Sugar, Candy
7th	Brass, Wool, Copper
8th	Pottery, Bronze
9th	Willow
10th	Tin
11th	Steel
12th	Silk, Linen
13th	Lace
14th	Ivory
15th	Crystal
20th	China
25th	Silver
30th	Pearl
35th	Coral
40th	Ruby
45th	Sapphire
50th	Gold
55th	Emerald
75th	Diamond

Source Materials

To the apprentice journalist writing his first story, the five questions—who, what, when, where, why—are always a challenge. The same questions can present quite a challenge to the display man when there is a sudden need for ostrich plumes, pin hammers, an inexpensive ball light fixture or giant poppies.

Competition, time and service will cause the popularity of the suppliers listed here to wax and wane, but they now offer much in the way of imaginative beginnings for better merchandise displays.

ALL-PURPOSE, BASIC SUPPLIERS
Austen Display, Inc., 133 W. 19th St., New York 11, N.Y.

James A. Cole Co., 235 Park Ave., S., New York 3, N.Y.

Elect Mfg. Co., Inc., 71–15A Grand Ave., Maspeth L.I., N.Y.

Garrison-Wagner Co., 2018 Washington Ave., St. Louis 3, Mo.

Melvin S. Roos & Co., Inc., 181 S. Pryor St., S.W., Atlanta, Ga.

Nesbit Industries, Inc., 1823 N. Milwaukee Ave., Chicago 7, Ill.

ARTIFICIAL FOLIAGE
Artificial Plant Co., 210 Bell St., Chagrin Falls, Ohio.

L. J. Charrot Co., Inc., 36–38 W. 37th St., New York 18, N.Y.

Cook & Meier, Inc., 2345 S. Michigan Ave., Chicago 16, Ill.

Display Associates, Inc., 930 Newark Ave., Jersey City 6, N.Y.

Metwood Floral Mfgrs., Inc., 109 Bloomsbury St., Trenton 10, N.J.

Oltmanns Co., 1405 Douglas Street, Omaha 2, Nebraska.

Schack's, Inc., 2516 W. Armitage Ave., Chicago 47, Ill.

FABRICS and RIBBONS
Cappel Display, 338 W. 4th St., Cincinnati, Ohio.

Central Shippee, Inc., 24 W. 25th St., New York 10, N.Y.

Maharam Fabric Corp., 130 W. 46th St., New York, 36, N.Y.

Park Lane Fabrics Co., Inc., 45 East 30th St., New York 16, N.Y.

Van Arden Fabrics, 43 W. 36th St., New York, N.Y.

W.E.R. Ribbon Corp., 440 Fourth Ave., New York, N.Y.

FIXTURES
American Display Fixture Co., 20 W. 27th St., New York 1, N.Y.

L. A. Darling Co., 606 N. Matteson St., Bronson, Mich.

Ferro-Craft, 305 W. Morton St., Morganfield, Ky.

National Form & Fixture Co., 87 Richardson St., Brooklyn 11, N.Y.

Nat Siegel, Inc., 39 W. 37th St., New York 18, N.Y.

Leo Prager, Inc., 153 W. 23rd St., New York 11, N.Y.

Thall Plastics & Metals, Inc., 139 Duane St., New York 13, N.Y.

IMPORTERS
Brunn & Bertheim, 1200 Broadway, New York 1, N.Y.

Display Marketers, Inc., N.W. Corner "A" & Clearfield Sts., Philadelphia 34, Pa.

Frankel Assoc., Inc., 56 W. 45th St., New York 36, N.Y.

Kaytee Imports, Inc., 28 W. 27th St., New York 1, N.Y.

Lombardo & Co., Inc., 1247 61st St., Brooklyn 19, N.Y.

Royal Cathay, 1201 Folsom St., San Francisco, Calif.

Royal Display Products, 48 W. 22nd St., New York 10, N.Y.

LIGHTING EQUIPMENT

Amplex Corp., 214 Glen Dove Rd., Carle Place, L.I., N.Y.

Black Light Products, 67 E. Lake St., Chicago 1, Ill.

Lustra Corporation of America, 40 W. 25th St., New York, N.Y.

McGinnis Bros., Inc., Box 442, Greenville, Pa.

Noel Mfg. Co., Inc., 3 W. 18th St., New York 11, N.Y.

Northcraft Lighting Corp., 12 Maple Ave., Haverstraw, N.Y.

Swivelier Co., Inc., Nanuet, N.Y.

Sylvania Electric Products, Inc., 1740 Broadway, New York 19, N.Y.

MAGAZINES and SERVICES

J. M. Biow Co., 475 Fifth Ave., New York 17, N.Y.

"Display," 120 St. Louis Ave., Fort Worth 1, Texas.

"Display World," 407 E. Gilbert St., Cincinnati 1, Ohio.

Retail Reporting Bureau, 101 Fifth Ave., New York 3, N.Y.

"Southern Display News," P.O. Box 743, Fort Worth 1, Texas.

"Views & Reviews," Milton B. Conhaim, Inc., 101 Fifth Ave., New York 3, N.Y.

Worsinger Window Service, 110 W. 40th St., New York 18, N.Y.

MANNEQUIN REPAIRS and WIGS

Arranjay's Wig Co., 34 W. 20th St., New York 11, N.Y.

Carter Mannequin Studio, 178 Broad St., S.W., Atlanta 3, Ga.

Emil Corsillo, Inc., 1343 N. LeBrea Ave., Hollywood 28, Calif.

Herzberg-Robbins, Inc., 457 West Broadway, New York 12, N.Y.

Mannequin Service & Repair Studio, 3104 S. Main St., Fort Worth, Texas.

Anna Mesa of Miami, 6710 N.W. 32nd Ave., Miami, Fla.

Santa Claus School, Inc., Christmas Park, Albion, N.Y.

MANNEQUINS

L. A. Darling Co., 606 N. Matteson St., Bronson, Mich.

Decter Mannikin Co., Inc., 1000 S. Los Angeles St., Los Angeles, Calif.

The Greneker Corp., 991 Sixth Ave., New York 18, N.Y.

Goldsmith & Sons, 207 W. 37th St., New York 18, N.Y.

Tero Inc., 153 W. 23rd St., New York 11, N.Y.

D. G. Williams, Inc., 498 Seventh Ave., New York 18, N.Y.

Wolf & Vine, Inc., 225 S. Los Angeles St., Los Angeles 12, Calif.

MOTION, SOUND SYSTEMS, RIDES, etc.

Alderman Associates, Inc., 298 Fifth Ave., New York 1, N.Y.

Amplifier Corp. of America, 396 Broadway, New York 13, N.Y.

Gale Dorothea Mechanisms, 81–101 Broadway, Elmhurst, N.Y.

Miniature Train Co., Rensselaer, Ind.

Noel Mfg. Co., Inc., 3 W. 18th St., New York 11, N.Y.

Rocket Express Systems, 219 N. Humphrey Ave., Oak Park, Ill.

Soundisplay Enterprises, 1997 Jerome Ave., Bronx 53, N.Y.

NATURAL FOLIAGE

Carolina Foliage Co., Mount Airy, North Carolina.

Display Effects, 721 Browder, Dallas, Texas.

Dave Starkman, 4426 Santa Monica Blvd., Los Angeles 29, Calif.

Spaeth Displays, Inc., 4–05 26th Ave., Astoria 2, L.I., N.Y.

PAPERS, MAT and CARDBOARD STOCK

Bulkley Dunton & Co., Inc., 9 Pennsylvania Ave., Corry, Pa.

Chicago Cardboard Co., 656 W. Washington Blvd., Chicago, Ill.

Duplex Display & Mfg. Co., 916 Arch St., Philadelphia 7, Pa.

W. C. Hurlock, Inc., 123 E. Baltimore Ave., Lansdowne, Pa.

Reyburn Mfg. Co., Inc., Royersford, Pa.

R-Tex Co., 41–45 Morris St., Jersey City 2, N.J.

Timbertone Decorative Co., Inc., 114 East 32nd St., New York 16, N.Y.

PROMOTIONAL DISPLAYS and SET PIECES

Allied Display Materials, Inc., 241 23rd St., New York 11, N.Y.

Bliss Display Corp., 37–21 32nd St., Long Island City 1, N.Y.

Decorative Plant Corp., 136 W. 24th St., New York 11, N.Y.

Earl W. Gasthoff Co., 112–116 N. Hazel St., Danville, Ill.

David Hamberger Inc., 136 W. 31st St., New York 1, N.Y.

Pacific Promotions, 1630 S. Flower St., Los Angeles 15, Calif.

Silvestri Art Mfg. Co., 1147 W. Ohio St., Chicago 22, Ill.

SHOP SUPPLIES

American Chemical Co., 207 N. Peters St., New Orleans, La.

Dick Blick, P.O. Box 469, Galesburg, Ill.

Devoe & Raynolds Co., Inc., 135 S. Wabash Ave., Chicago, Ill.

G. C. Dom Supply Company, 125 East Pearl St., Kansas City, Mo.

International Register Co., 2622 W. Washington Blvd., Chicago, Ill.

E. A. Lallemand & Son, 121 Second Ave. N., Nashville, Tenn.

Leo Uhlfelder & Co., 159 W. 25th St., New York, N.Y.

SIGNS, MURALS, TOPPERS, etc.

Display Equipment Corp., 147 W. 37th St., New York 18, N.Y.

Morgan Sign Machine Co., 4510 N. Ravenswood Ave., Chicago 40, Ill.

Moss Photo Studio, 155 W. 45th St., New York, N.Y.

Resident Display Inc., 155 Waverly Place, New York 14, N.Y.

Reynolds Printasign Co., 9830 San Fernando Rd., Pacoima, Calif.

Showcard Machine Co., 320 W. Ohio St., Chicago 10, Ill.

W. L. Stensgaard & Asso., Inc., 346 N. Justine St., Chicago, Ill.

STORE DIRECTORIES and LETTERS

Acme Bulletin Co., 37 East 12th St., New York 3, N.Y.

Arkow-Lewis, 705 Arch St., Philadelphia, Pa.

Bulletin Boards & Directory Products, Inc., 724 Broadway, New York 3, N.Y.

Display Craft, 963 Lake Drive, S.E., Grand Rapids 6, Mich.

Jay-Gee Studio, 434 Sixth Ave., New York 11, N.Y.

Mitten's Display Letters, 39 W. 60th St., New York 23, N.Y.

Scott Plastics Co., 805–11 Tenth St., Palmetto, Florida.

W. L. Stensgaard & Associates, Inc., 346 N. Justine St., Chicago 7, Ill.

Bibliography

Unfortunately there just are not enough good books available on display. The real greats in the working field today (and in the past) are too busy with current problems and pressures to take the time to write more than sparingly on their art. But the treatises herewith suggested are certainly a bright beginning until more is forthcoming from the pens of such eminences as Lester Gaba, George Payne, Al Bliss, Henry Callahan and Gene Moore.

Benson and Carey, *The Elements of Lettering*. New York: McGraw-Hill, 1950.

Bernard, Frank, *Dynamic Display*. Cincinnati: Display World, 1962.

Birren, Faber, *Selling with Color*. New York: McGraw-Hill.

Birren, Faber, *Selling Color to People*. New York: University Books, 1956.

Buckley, Jim, *The Drama of Display*. New York: Pellegrini & Cudahy, 1953.

Carboni, Erberto, *Exhibitors and Displays*. New York: Graphic, 1959.

Castro, Nestor, *Handbook of Window Display*. Hastings, 1953.

Chord, J. T., *Window Display Manual*. Cincinnati: Display Publishing Company, 1931.

Coffin, Harry B., *Art Archives*. New York: New York Press, 1950.

Cowee, Howard, N.A.D.I. *Visual Merchandising Research Series*. New York: Prentice-Hall, 1950.

Curtis, Frieda, *How to Give a Fashion Show*. New York: Fairchild Publications, 1950.

Davis, Deering, *Contemporary Decor*. New York: Architectural Book Publishing Co., 1950.

East, Marjorie, *Display for Learning: Making and Using Visual Materials*. New York: Dryden Press, 1952.

Fernandez, Jose A., *The Specialty Shop*. New York: Architectural Book Publishing Co., 1950.

Gaba, Lester, *The Art of Window Display*. New York: The Studio Publications, 1952.

Gallico, Paul, *Mrs. 'Arris Goes to Paris*. Garden City, New York: Doubleday & Co., 1958.

Gardner and Heller, *Exhibitions and Display*. New York: McGraw, 1960.

Herdeg, Walter, *Window Display*. Praeger.

Herndon, Booton, *Bergdorf's on the Plaza*. New York: Alfred A. Knopf, 1956.

Hurst, A. E., *Displaying Merchandise for Profit*. New York: Prentice-Hall, 1939.

Kimbrough, Emily, *Through Charley's Door*. New York: Harper, 1952.

Kretschmer, Robert, *Window and Interior Display*. Scranton: Laurel Publishers, 1952.

Lehner, Ernest, *Symbols, Signs and Signets*. New York: World Publishing Co., 1950.

Leydenfrost, Robert, *Window Display*. New York: Architectural Book Publishing Co., 1950.

Loomis, Andrew, *Fun With a Pencil*. New York: The Viking Press, 1939.

Martine, Herbert E., *Color*. Pelham: Bridgman Publishers, 1928.

Merchant's Service. The National Cash Register Co., Dayton, Ohio. No-charge pamphlets on request.

Moore, P. G., *Principles of Merchandise Display*. Austin, Texas: University of Texas, 1945.

Nesbitt, Alexander, *Lettering*. New York: Prentice-Hall, 1950.

Picken, J. H., *Principles of Window Display*. New York: McGraw-Hill, 1927.

Sadler, Arthur, *Paper Sculpture*. Pitman, 1955.

Zaidenberg, Arthur, *Anyone Can Draw*. New York: World Publishing Co., 1939.